PRAYING

with

BODY

and

SOUL

A Way to Intimacy with God

Jane E. Vennard

Augsburg
MINNEAPOLIS

PRAYING WITH BODY AND SOUL

Scripture quotations from the New Revised Standard Version of the Bible are copyright © 1989 by the Division of Christian Education of the National Council of Churches of Christ in the United States of America and are used by permission.

Cover design: Mike Mihelich
Cover image: David Ash/Tony Stone Images. Used by permission.
Interior design: Julie Odland Smith

Library of Congress Cataloging-in-Publication Data

Vennard, Jane E. (Jane Elizabeth), 1940–
    Praying with body and soul : a way to intimacy with God / Jane E.
Vennard
        p.   cm.
    Includes bibliographical references.
    ISBN 0-8066-3614-9
    1. Prayer—Christianity.   I. Title.
BV210.2.V46   1998
248.3'2—dc21

The paper used in this publication meets the minimum requirements of American National Standard for Information Sciences—Permanence of Paper for Printed Library Materials, ANSI Z329.48-1984.   ∞ ™

Manufactured in the U.S.A.   AF 9–3614

02   01   00   99   2   3   4   5   6   7   8   9   10

CONTENTS

for Jim

ACKNOWLEDGMENTS

In the fall of 1993 I enrolled in a dance class. I did not know exactly what I was signing up for; I simply knew that I was longing for movement. What I discovered was a spiritual practice that grounded my love of God in my body, released my creativity, and taught me the truth about surrender. In these five years I have learned to "sweat my prayers" through the work of Gabrielle Roth as taught to me and others by Chris Donovan. This book grows from the moist and fertile ground of my movement practice.

Ronald Klug, director of publishing for Augsburg Books, accepted my book proposal. He then became my editor. With a minimum number of words and a maximum amount of trust, he guided my creative process. His casual suggestions, his well-placed appreciations, his lack of urgency, and his fine eye for the written word have helped make this book the one you hold in your hands.

Many others have helped me write clearly. Craig Vittetoe, my high school English teacher, taught me grammar and research skills that have served me well. Beth Gaede, my editor for *Praying for Friends and Enemies*, guided me in the fine art of writing for publication. Jim Laurie and Sharyl Peterson read this manuscript with loving hearts and clear and critical minds, offering important suggestions. Carla Ficke and Doree Bauerline read for accuracy of content and to weed out subtle bias.

Completing a manuscript takes the hard work of practical tasks. Cathie Woehl, my secretary, has been strong and faithful through the entire project. She has typed and retyped and typed again as sections and chapters rearranged themselves and as I struggled for the right sentence order, the correct word, the perfect phrase. My student assistant, Kay Young, accomplished the tedious task of completing accurately the notes and the suggested reading list. We are both grateful to Paul Millette of the Iliff School of Theology library for his help in searching out elusive sources.

Many people have unknowingly contributed to this book by stimulating a thought over coffee, speaking of their own experiences over lunch, or quoting an author who illustrated a point I was trying to make. For these unexpected gifts I thank Stephanie West Allen, Siri Everet, Margaret Johnson,

Jamie Laurie, John Lee, Mark Meeks, Daniel O'Connor, Ruth Robinson, and Vie Thorgren.

I am grateful for the many beautiful and sacred places in which I was able to think and pray and write undisturbed. Most of this book was written at the Columbine Ranch in Jefferson, Colorado. I deeply appreciate the generosity of Swanee Hunt and the hospitality of Barb and Al Reynolds. I also found welcome and inspiration at the Sacred Heart Retreat House in Sedalia, Colorado; the Christian Prayer Retreat House in Idaho Springs, Colorado; and the Grandview Cabin in Cripple Creek, Colorado.

The people of my home church, Sixth Avenue United Church of Christ, supported my writing with their encouragement and their prayers. A small group met with me in the early stages of my creative process to brainstorm ideas, make suggestions, and give me feedback on early drafts. Many of their ideas have been incorporated into this finished work. To speak and teach while I am writing is invaluable in my creative process. The following churches welcomed my work-in-progress in adult education classes, retreats, or prayer days: Calvary Baptist Church of Denver, Central Presbyterian Church of Denver, First Congregational Church of Colorado Springs, First Congregational United Church of Christ of Ogallala, Nebraska, First Universalist Church of Denver, Grace United Methodist Church of Denver, Hope United Methodist Church of Englewood, Colorado, Lakewood United Church of Christ of Lakewood, Colorado, St. Andrew United Methodist Church of Littleton, Colorado, St. John's Episcopal Church of Boulder, Colorado, and University Congregational Church of Seattle, Washington.

Finally, and most important, this book could not have been written without the stories, experiences, dreams, and journeys of directees, students, retreatants, and friends who have graced my life. The storytellers of chapter 3—Trish Dunn, Brian LeMaire, Nancy Eckburg, Roy Loats, and Karen Lowe—had the courage to trust me, and ultimately you, with their physical and spiritual struggles and victories. The other chapters are filled with the words, ideas, examples, actions, questions and prayers of an unknown number of seekers. Some stories have been disguised to protect privacy. Other stories have been presented to you as they were told or written to me. For these people, named and unnamed, I offer a prayer of thanksgiving.

INTRODUCTION
Praying with Body and Soul

When I was growing up, I believed that prayer was asking God for something I wanted or telling God what had happened to me during the week. Prayer seemed a little pointless because I rarely got what I wanted and I was pretty sure that with all the major events going on in the world God could not be too concerned with the rejection I felt when I wasn't invited to Mary's party.

I was also confused by the Lord's Prayer, which I had memorized. I understood the request for daily bread, but what did "hallowed be thy name" mean? And what were my "debts"? Being "delivered from evil" was frightening, for the phrase indicated that evil was near. And "the kingdom, power, and glory" had nothing to do with my life. I was twelve years old, living in a Christian family, attending church and Sunday school regularly, praying as I had been taught, but I had no experience of God being active in my life. God seemed like a good idea; I believed in God. I even had faith that God loved me, but God seemed very far away, terribly vague, and something to attend to on Sundays.

As I grew older, I sensed I was missing something; I sensed there was something more. I began to feel a longing for God to be closer—for God to be a companion, a constant presence in my life. I came to long for an intimate relationship with God. I imagined being silent with God and knowing God through all my senses. I imagined laughing and crying and playing and dancing with God. And most startling, I began to wonder if God was also longing for me.

My longings and my wonderings were affirmed through a variety of sources and experiences. I recalled the parable in the Gospel of Luke about the woman searching for a lost coin (15:8-10), and I began to believe that God *was* searching for me and would rejoice when I was found. I discovered the closeness of God through the prophet Jeremiah quoting God as saying, "Before I formed you in the womb I knew you" (1:5).

I remembered when my father died and I couldn't cry until a man who had been my father's friend took me in his arms. I wept and wept, feeling safe and warm, and I was comforted as this loving man wept with me. I wondered if this comfort mirrored God's love for me. I remembered times by the ocean when I had been stopped by a sunset, or one simple, perfect seashell, or the cry of a gull, and had known, like Moses, that I was standing "on holy ground."

I watched with wonder people sitting cross-legged and perfectly still, deep in Buddhist meditation. I sensed the delight of the whirling Sufi dancers. I marveled at the peace I saw in the faces of people silently praying the rosary as the beads slipped through their fingers.

I heard about Hildegard of Bingen, an eleventh-century Christian mystic, scientist, artist, and musician who drew on the experience of nature to describe the spirit of God. Observing the wonder of nature's push to life in springtime, seeing the greening of the world as a symbol of life, she called God *veriditas*, which is translated as "greening." God for Hildegard was a verb, an action, a process, a power to bring new life to all the world. I read a choreopoem by Ntozake Shange in which a character claims: "i found God in myself & i loved her, i loved her fiercely." Recently I read *Life of the Beloved* by Henri Nouwen, a contemporary Catholic writer who, in a letter, told a friend and all of us that we are all the beloved daughters or sons of God.

Through the many years since my childhood I have been searching for an intimate relationship with God. I have been led by my longings and my own experiences. I have been guided by the writings of Hebrew and Christian scriptures and Church mothers and fathers. I have been delighted and challenged by the written and spoken stories of others who search for God. I have discovered new images and new ideas in the work of poets and novelists, psychologists and theologians.

I am writing this book to share with you how my understanding, experience, and practice of prayer have opened and expanded since I was a child. My prayer now includes silence and stillness, movement and imagination, sensuality and sexuality, laughter and play, work, service, and the struggle for justice. Prayer has become for me the practice of bringing all of who I have been, all of who I am, and all of who I am becoming into relationship with God. When I bring all of myself to God, I am praying with body and soul.

I am writing this book from the midst of my searching. My longings have not been fully satisfied and my journey has not ceased. I continue to be led and guided, delighted and challenged by experiences, stories, insights, and unanswerable questions. I hope that in some way this book might serve to stir your own longings for God, encourage the process of your own searching, and deepen your spirituality.

Spirituality is a term often used in conjunction with *prayer*, and it needs to be clarified because it is used in so many ways. My definition of *spiritual* is "all that has to do with one's relationship with God." Therefore the *spiritual* life is a life, all of life, lived in relationship with God. A *spiritual* practice is that which we do to deepen and strengthen our relationship with God. A *spiritual* retreat is time away from the busy-ness of everyday life to spend intentional time in relationship with God. A *spiritual* reading is any book or poem or story that may guide us in our relationship to God. A *spiritual* teacher is any person who helps us see ways of relating to God. Spirituality is about growing, weaving, deepening, strengthening, and embracing fully our relationship to God. And prayer is at the heart of that relationship.

The way in which I imagine God will be central to how I live my spiritual life. If God is "out there," I will be building my relationship with another. If God is "within me," I will be seeking a loving relationship with my Self. If I see God embodied in my sisters and brothers, I will begin weaving right relationships with those around me. If I see God in Jesus, I will be searching for a clearer relationship with him. If I see God manifest in all of creation, I will desire to relate lovingly with all living things. If I see God in *all* these images, my spiritual life will include learning more and more about relating to God in a variety of ways.

I believe our relationship with God is initiated by God. God is searching for us, longing for us, "wooing" us. Whenever and however we respond to God's call to relationship we are in prayer. Understanding prayer as response rather than initiation makes the experience of prayer easier for me. Remember being a teenager and needing to call someone to invite him or her to a party or a dance? The call was not just about an activity; the call was about relationship: "Will you go with me?" "Will you be with me?" "Will you accept me?" Those phone calls were always hard for me. I was never sure what to say; I was afraid of rejection. I was mostly afraid that the person on the other end of the line would say, "Jane? Jane who?" Because of my fear I often did not make the call. On the other hand, if someone called to invite me to an activity, my response came easily. I had words, I had ideas, I could make decisions. Responding was much easier than inviting.

This difficulty of initiating and the ease of responding are also true with God. When I anticipate calling on God, I do not know how to begin, I am not sure what to say, my words always seem to be flat and uninteresting. I begin to wonder if God cares about me at all. And then (the greatest of fears) what if I call on God after a long absence and God replies, "Jane who?" But believing that God is calling to me, that God wants to be in relationship with me, that God knows who I am and what I need, my responses come more easily. I am free to respond to God with body and soul. When we pray with body and soul we respond to God with all of who we are. There is no part of ourselves or our experience that we do not bring into our relationship with God.

We know in human relationships that the more of ourselves we bring to relationship the more honest, the more fulfilling, the richer the relationship can be. When we do not express anger to a friend, we withhold a vital part of ourself and put the relationship at risk. When we do not take our laughter and delight to a party we find ourselves bored or boring. If we deny the needs of the child within, our relationships are likely to become serious and flat. We know this in relationship to others. How much more true it is with God! God in God's fullness welcomes us in our fullness into relationship and loving embrace. How rich this sacred relationship can become if we are willing to respond completely and unconditionally, with all of who we are.

Praying with body and soul leads us away from a "stripped-down" spirituality in which we relate to God with pious words, soft voices, and polite responses and into a large, expansive, embodied, grounded, imaginative spirituality in which we are free to shout and rage at God, question God, laugh with God, dance with God, push God away, chase after God, and ultimately fall in love with God. Praying with body and soul allows a robust intimacy to develop between ourselves and God.

Biblical Stories of Praying with Body and Soul

To understand the possibility of deep intimacy with God, reflect on the ancient story of Jacob wrestling with God (Genesis 32:22-32). Jacob and an unknown man wrestled until daybreak. "When the man saw he did not prevail against Jacob, he struck him on the hip socket; and Jacob's hip was put out of joint as he wrestled with him" (v. 25). Then the two wrestled verbally, asking each other for names, and Jacob requested a blessing which was at first withheld. When he was finally renamed and blessed, Jacob said: "I have seen God face-to-face" (v. 30).

The Psalms are also examples of body and soul prayers, because they are filled with emotions and imagination. The psalmist is often fearful and angry and willing to shout at God. In Psalm 35 the psalmist is angry that the Lord has been silent and has not come to his rescue. He prays:

> You have seen, O Lord; do not be silent!
>   O Lord, do not be far from me!
> Wake up! Bestir yourself for my defense. . . .
> (Ps. 35:22-23)

When the psalmist rejoices, there is no limit to his celebration and praise:

> I give you thanks, O Lord, with my whole heart;
>   before the gods I sing your praise;
> I bow down toward your holy temple
>   and give thanks to your name for your
>   steadfast love and your faithfulness. . . .
> (Ps. 138:1-2)

And when the psalmist responds to God's call to relationship he responds with languages and images that reflect all of who he is:

> I listen for you; my soul listens like a deer
> in the forest.
> My soul waits more intently than a soldier
> watching for the dawn.
> (Ps. 130:5-6)[1]

In Christian scriptures, the story of the poor widow is a prayer of body and soul, and Jesus recognized it as such (Luke 12:41-44). As he sat by the treasury, Jesus watched the crowd contributing large sums of money. In the midst of this wealthy group, a poor widow came forth to give two small copper coins which were worth a penny. Jesus called his disciples together and said: "Truly I tell you, this poor widow has put in more than all those who are contributing to the treasury. For all of them have contributed out of their abundance; but she out of her poverty has put in everything she had . . . " (vv. 43-44).

Jesus prayed with body and soul, all of himself engaged in his relationship with God. Imagine the prayers of forty days in the wilderness, tempted by Satan, accompanied by wild beasts and waited on by angels (Mark 1:12-13). Imagine Jesus' long night in Gethsemane with his disciples asleep: Jesus agonizing over what had happened, and finally letting go into God (Mark 14:32-42). Hear the words of his final prayer: "My God, my God, why have you forsaken me?" (Mark 15:34b). These are prayer experiences pulled from the depth of Jesus' being, prayers of his body and soul.

The Reformed tradition follows the biblical examples of praying with body and soul in the first question and answer of the Heidelberg Catechism:

> Q: What is your only comfort in life and in death?
> A: That I belong—
>   body and soul,
>   in life and in death—
> not to myself but
> to my faithful Savior, Jesus Christ. . . . [2]

Throughout this book I will use the phrase "body and soul" to denote all of who we are: our physicality, our emotions, our intuitions, our imaginations, our minds and all of our experiences—past, present, and future. Therefore, when we pray with body and soul, or love with body and soul, or belong with body and soul, we are believing, responding, surrendering with all of who we are.

Although I write from a Christian perspective for a primarily Christian audience and use much of the language of my tradition, I believe that praying with body and soul transcends religious belief. Whatever the images or the languages or practices, all religions speak of the longing for relationship with God. Nontheistic religions and belief systems speak of the longing for peaceful and loving relationships with oneself, one's neighbor and all of creation.

I hope that my Christian readers will discover an opening in their prayer life that will allow for greater understanding of people of other faiths. I hope that readers of other faith traditions will hear in these thoughts and stories the longing for connection and unity with whatever they call holy. May all of us come to believe that we are being called into loving relationship, and that it is possible for all of us, whoever we may be, to respond with body and soul.

How to Use This Book

In this book I will tell stories about, suggest opportunities for, and describe ways of relating to God with all of who we are. The purpose of the suggestions and descriptions is not so much to teach you how to pray as to help you recognize the many and varied ways you are already praying. I assume you are already relating to God in some personal and intense ways, but may not have called all these experiences "prayer." When the concept of prayer is opened to include all the ways we respond to God's call, and all the ways we nurture our relationship to God, people are often amazed at how much they are already praying and how much they already know about prayer. I trust this book will lead you to a similar experience and will affirm your relationship with God.

Chapter 1 pays attention to the wisdom of our bodies and how our bodies can teach us, if we listen, about new ways to be in prayer. The stories and suggestions will guide us toward a positive relationship with our physical nature so that we can accept our bodies as our teachers.

Knowing and relating to God through all our senses is the focus of chapter 2. Our "sensual spirituality" leads to a discussion of sexuality; we will seek to understand why Christians have been afraid to include their sexuality as an integral part of their relationship to God. We will discover how our sensuality and sexuality can guide us in prayer.

Chapter 3 attends to our imperfect bodies. We too often celebrate the wonder of the body and do not address the reality of damaged body images, negative body experiences, accidents, aging, illness, and death. No exploration of the body and soul in prayer is complete without looking at the experience of having our bodies betray us.

Reinhold Niebuhr said, "Humor is the prelude to faith, and laughter the beginning of prayer." Chapter 4 brings fun and laughter and play and delight to the foreground of our relationship with God. Why do we take prayer so seriously? How can we release our childlike wonder and delight and let it guide us into a deeper relationship with God?

Chapter 5 explores the wonder of the imagination and how our ability to imagine can draw us more deeply into prayer. We will discuss images of the soul, imagining details, people and events in Bible stories, and paying attention to our dream images. We will play with how our images of God can limit or expand our prayers.

Chapter 6 focuses on the image of the person, which includes our many self-images and the mystery of who we are. As God can be named in many ways, so too can we, who are made in God's image. When we experience ourselves as complex and rich, we may be surprised to learn how our many parts can lead us more fully into prayer.

Contemplation and action are at the center of chapter 7. We will explore how they are connected through work, service, and the struggle for justice. We will discover ways to pray that place our bodies and souls in the midst of human suffering. We will balance the spiritual gifts we receive from creation with our responsibility to care for the earth.

We cannot be Christians alone. Chapter 8 will explore ways we can bring our individual relationship with God into community, and ways church can strengthen our lives of prayer, work, and service. Through membership in the body of Christ we discover the true meaning of the great commandment: "You shall love the Lord your God with all your heart, with all your soul, and with all your strength and with all your mind; and your neighbor as yourself" (Luke 10:27).

You can use this book in a variety of ways. You may wish to read it on your own, reflecting as you go on the ways your relationship with God has grown, developed, and changed over the years. The activities designed for reflection and discussion will help you personally experience new ways to pray and move the ideas off the pages and into your body and soul. You might read and study this material with a prayer partner, sharing your journeys as you go, guiding each other through the activities, and reflecting together on the ways you could expand and embrace your relationship with God.

Praying with Body and Soul is also designed for group study. My hope is that the ideas and stories and activities will guide group participants not only to a discussion of the material, but to a sharing of their own personal prayer experiences. Over the years we have taken Jesus' words about praying in secret (Matt. 6:6) too literally. People are willing to talk about many personal things but are reluctant to speak openly about prayer. Speaking about our own experiences of prayer not only helps us to clarify and deepen our own thoughts, feelings, and physical experiences of God, but also serves others by expanding their understanding of the limitless possibilities of prayer experiences. In addition, a group willing to share their personal experiences of prayer deepen their relationships with each other as well as with God. The Group Study Guide is designed to facilitate this process.

As you read and reflect, embrace and discard, taste and experience the material in this book, my prayer for you is that your journey with and toward God will be nourished, that your experience of prayer will be expanded, and that your own unique spirituality will be affirmed. May you proceed with a lively mind, a light heart, and a willing body, open to the wonder of God's love for you.

1

OUR BODIES TEACH US TO PRAY

What do many of us do with our bodies when someone says "Let us pray?" There is a moment of rustling as we stop what we are in the midst of doing, then a collective silence as we bow our heads. Sometimes hands come together in laps, sometimes folded in front of chests, sometimes with palms open on knees. The one who is about to pray usually waits until everyone is in this position before beginning the words of invocation or petition or thanksgiving.

As children, we learned this prayer position from watching adults. If we were slow to catch on we were taught by words or gestures. Sometimes the worship leader gave the instructions, "Please bow your heads in prayer." "Shhh! Be quiet! Bow your head," whispered a parent. An older sister grabbed the hands of her little brother and slapped them together in front of his chest then pushed his head down. When it popped up she pushed it down again, becoming his self-appointed instructor in the proper ways of prayer. However we learned this prayer position, it became as automatic as the response to a stop sign and as quick as the reactions of the students and teachers in my California school of the 1950s who dove for cover under their desks at the sound of the earthquake siren.

Kneeling is another prayer position commonly taught in the Christian tradition. Congregations may kneel together at certain points in a service. Individuals may kneel in prayer at the communion rail or at their places after communion. Some children are taught to kneel at their bedsides for evening prayers. Many adults will fall to their knees in private when they are moved to certain forms of prayer. When we place our bodies in these familiar positions we ready our souls for prayer. In other words, we have taught our bodies and souls how to pray.

What might happen if we reversed this standard procedure of teaching the body and allowed the body to teach us? To do this we must let go of the idea that the mind alone has knowledge the body needs, and recognize the unique knowledge the body contains. We can turn our attention to our bodies and see what *they* have to say. If we are willing to listen, we will find that our bodies have amazing lessons and quiet wisdom to share.

The Body as Teacher

To allow the body to become your teacher of prayer, place your body in a new position, one that you may have not have associated with prayer. For example, you might stand and tilt your head back slightly so you are looking up. Raise your arms to waist level and open them wide as if you were about to welcome a loved one into your embrace. Allow your eyes to close. Hold this posture gently, breathing in the experience of your body, and listen to the prayer that begins to form in your soul. Your prayer may come in words or images, snatches of music, or a physical sensation of moving more deeply into relationship with God. Listen and trust what comes. Truly, the body knows how to pray.

An infinite number of prayer sites and positions are available to us. We can be inside or outside, alone or in community. We can sit, kneel, stand, walk, lie down. We can bow our heads, raise our heads, or look straight into the world. We can open our eyes wide or close them tight or hold a soft gaze in which our eyelids are lowered but not quite closed. Our hands can be folded, pressed palm to palm, or simply open on our laps or at our sides. Our arms can dangle or lift up or reach out. If we are in a group, we can hold hands. Each position we choose will allow the body to teach us something new about prayer.

When the body teaches us to pray, our relationship to God is expanded and deepened. When the body teaches us to pray, we realize we can pray at any time without having to stop to sit quietly and bow our heads. When the body teaches us to pray, many new prayer forms are open to us. Listen to what a variety of people have learned from their bodies about prayer:

"When I opened my eyes and reached out to hold the hands of my neighbors, my prayers shifted from my individual relationship with God to my relationship with my sisters and brothers, and I was filled with gratitude for being part of the human family and this community in particular."

"I always thought I had to sit still to be praying. When I learned to listen to my body I asked it how it might pray when I swim. As I moved back and forth the length of the pool—breathing, stroking, breathing, stroking—I discovered I was chanting. I was repeating rhythmically a phrase that coincided with my breathing patterns. Now the pool has become a sacred place. I go there to be with God body and soul."

"I have never knelt in prayer. But when I got down on my knees, I discovered a depth of prayer not known before. Somehow this position allowed me to truly know my radical dependence on God."

"Lying on my back with my eyes closed, I felt held in God's loving embrace. I was cherished. I was safe."

"I became aware how difficult it is to open my heart when my hands are clenched. Now I always open my hands when I pray. I seem to be more able to feel the spirit moving in my life."

"My breath is restricted when I bow my head. No matter what the minister says, I lift my chin slightly and gaze at the cross behind the altar. My experience of God's presence in worship has become more real."

Our bodies do not need to be particularly agile or active to be vibrant teachers of prayer. A woman flat on her back recovering from an injury found forms of prayer she had never known: "I was always running around so fast I would pray 'on the fly.' With my body immobilized I have discovered the blessing of stillness." An elderly man stopped coming to the communion rail. When the pastor asked him why, he replied, "I can no longer kneel. I am unable to receive the sacraments in any other position." His pastor replied, "Come to the rail. Kneel in your heart. God will know you are on your knees." This compassionate response engaged his imagination and freed his body to do and be what it was, and, most important, returned this man to full participation in the sacrament.

Prayer of the Heart

During a day of prayer that included attending to the body with reverence, I led the participants through a meditation on the heart. We placed our hands over our hearts, feeling them beating. We found our pulse in various places in our bodies, feeling the blood pumping through our systems. As we placed our hands gently on our bodies we gave thanks for the wonder of our hearts and the life that our blood carried throughout our bodies. We imagined the blood reaching the tips of our fingers and we gave thanks. We imagined the blood circulating through our brains and we gave thanks. We attended to the heart beating and pulsing on its own with no direction or control from us, and we gave thanks. The mystery of our bodies became a wonder to us and we thanked God for our embodiment and our lives.

One of the participants told me later that he was a heart surgeon. "Oh, my," I thought. "What did this sophisticated physician think of our simple and childlike exploration of the heart?" I did not need to worry, for he thanked me. He said he had reawakened to the glory of this organ, which he had grown to view as simply a problematic object to be fixed. "I had lost touch with the wonder of the heart," he said. "This brief meditation reminded me of what I know and what I do not know."

A Russian pilgrim who traveled across Russia in the tenth century in search of the meaning of Paul's instructions to pray always discovered that our hearts can teach us to pray without ceasing. In his travels he met many teachers, some of whom were helpful, some of whom were not. But he himself found that if he repeated a simple prayer over and over again, day after day, the prayer would move from his mouth and his mind into his heart. Once in the heart, the prayer would pray itself every second of every day as his heart beat steadily on. The pilgrim used the phrase, "Lord Jesus Christ, Son of God, have mercy on me, a sinner," which he believed to be the essence of the Gospels.[1]

Modern pilgrims have told me that this form of prayer is very helpful to them. They like having a prayer phrase ready. They feel their heart beating during the day and remember they are praying. And they delight when unexpectedly the phrase rises from their hearts to their minds or lips.

Some people have changed the prayer phrase to fit their own image of God and their own specific needs, for example: "Jesus, my brother, heal me," "Holy Spirit, console me," or "Gracious God, give me peace." Others have shared that the repeated phrase they use is a musical phrase. Sometimes the music stands alone and sometimes it contains the words of a hymn or a chant. Whatever the content of the prayer phrase, our praying hearts can guide us ever more constantly into the presence of God.

Breath Prayer

Our breath is as constant and as close as our hearts. In and out, in and out, in and out, the breath of life is continually refreshing and restoring us. We often take our breath for granted, so let us honor our breathing by pausing for a moment and offering a prayer of gratitude for the breath of life. Read through the following meditation and prayer so you can see where it is going, then if you are willing, settle yourself comfortably with your book in a position that leaves your hands free.

> When you are ready, take a few deep breaths and attend gently to both the inhalation and the exhalation. Place one hand near your nose and mouth so you can feel the breath going in and out . . . in and out. . . . Place your other hand on your chest so you can feel the gentle rise and fall of your lungs. . . . Play with deep and shallow breaths, slow and fast breaths, feeling your lungs expand and contract. . . . Gradually begin to imagine that each breath moves beyond your lungs into your entire body. Follow your breath down into your belly . . . into your legs . . . all the way to your

toes. . . . Imagine your breath filling your shoulders . . . flowing down your arms and into your hands and fingertips. . . . Imagine your breath soothing and easing your neck . . . circulating through your brain . . . massaging the space behind your eyes.

As you feel your breath in every part of your being, breathe a prayer of thanksgiving for the breath of life. . . . Be aware of the abundance of air . . . the ease with which it flows . . . and how little thought you have to give to this life-giving gift. Discover a phrase you can pray to the rhythm of your breathing, such as, "The breath of life; I give thanks. The breath of life; I give thanks. The breath of life; I give thanks." Stay with your breathing and praying as long as you wish. . . . Then close your prayer in any way that seems right.

As we attend to the wonder of our breathing, our breath itself can become a prayer. When we are upset, out of sorts, confused, distracted, or in any other state of mind and heart that seems to place us "beside ourselves," we can simply turn our attention to our breathing—in and out, in and out, in and out. This attention serves to remind us of the closeness of the spirit, the wonder of life, and the longing of God to be in relationship with us. As we remember who and whose we are, we might imagine we are breathing out whatever is bothering us and breathing in whatever we need. Like the prayer of the heart, breath prayer is constantly with us, readily available, and simple to do in any circumstance or situation. When we pay attention, our bodies teach us the constancy and closeness of God.

Reading the Bible Inside Out

Our bodies are also excellent Bible teachers, helping us get inside particular stories. When we physically participate in an event, we learn more than we would if we were simply to observe the action. It is hard to learn to swim without getting in the water! So it is with Bible stories. When we enter into the story with body and soul, we will discover new depths to familiar words.

Take for example the story of the bent-over woman in Luke 13:10-13. In this story, Jesus is teaching in the synagogue on the Sabbath. A woman appears who has been crippled for eighteen years. She is bent over and unable to stand up straight. Jesus calls her to him and lays his hands upon her, and she stands up tall and begins praising God. The religious leaders who see what has happened seem to dismiss the miracle of healing and take vehement exception to Jesus' healing on the Sabbath.

When we hear or read this story, we may think about how it would feel to be so crippled, we may wonder at the healing power of Jesus, or we may think about the conflict over obeying the laws of the sabbath. We may even place this story in the context of the whole Gospel, knowing that the tension between Jesus and the synagogue leaders is growing, and knowing this tension will lead Jesus to Jerusalem, betrayal and death.

Reading and thinking about Bible stories helps us to understand the meaning of the words and the events. We bring all our knowledge to a passage and we think seriously about what is being said. We may wonder what this passage can teach us about our lives today. When we read with our knowledge, our thoughts, and our wonderings, we are reading with our minds. We are reading the Bible from the outside in. This is the most common way to read the Bible. It is a good way, but it is not the only way.

To read Bible stories from the inside out we must engage our bodies and our imaginations. Go back to the words, "She is bent over and unable to stand up straight." As you read these words, bend your own body over at the waist, as far as you can go. Where do you put this book? Can you continue to read? What happens to your breathing? What can you see? Stay in this position for a minute or two. How does your body feel? As you do, imagine what it would be like to be bent over for eighteen years. If you are able, experiment with getting up and moving around still bent over at the waist.

Then imagine Jesus' presence. Imagine him calling to you. Move your body as if you were going to him. Feel his hands laid gently upon you. Slowly begin to straighten, experiencing the sensations in your body and soul. As you stand up straight, imagine how you would praise God.

A number of students discovered new and surprising prayers of praise pulled out of them when they experienced themselves as the crippled woman who received from Jesus the gift of new life:

> Oh my God! I am free!
> Life is wonderful—I can see!
> Thank you, bless you. I am free!

Dear God, thank you, thank you. I raise my hand and lift my head to praise you. I feel light and thrilled that you would help me. I am pleased, happy, undeserving. I am a new person who is going out to shout your glory to the world. Let us all praise you.

> Oh great gratitude—I can see the sky.
> I can breathe freely once again.
> I was so weary, but now I am released.
> My burden is lifted. Blessed be.

Thank you, O God. Thank you for giving me this freedom. You have delivered me. You have given me breath and life. I rejoice in you. I bask in your life. I will feel your touch on my head and my shoulder forever

and ever. I know you will always be with me and I will remember you
from this day on.

When we move inside a Bible story with our imaginations and our bodies, we do not dismiss our minds. We still struggle to understand the meaning of the passage. But we have new and different knowledge to bring to our
exploration. Having experienced the miracle of healing, we read and experience the rest of the passage in a new way. When we read how Jesus
answered the leader of the synagogue, the words become more than an intellectual debate over the keeping of the sabbath, because for a moment, by
becoming the woman in the story, we have become a daughter of Abraham
and the words are about us!

> "You hypocrites! Does not each of you on the sabbath untie his ox or his
> donkey from the manger, and lead it away to give it water? And ought not
> this woman, a daughter of Abraham whom Satan bound for eighteen long
> years, be set free from this bondage on the sabbath day?"

The healing of blind Bartimaeus (Mark 10:46-52) is another interesting
story to read from the inside out. In this story Bartimaeus is sitting begging
by the side of the road on the outskirts of Jericho when Jesus and his disciples and a large crowd pass by as they leave the city. Bartimaeus shouts out
to Jesus saying, "Jesus, son of David, have mercy on me!" When
Bartimaeus is sternly ordered to be quiet, he does not heed the warning and
shouts again, "Son of David, have mercy on me!" Jesus hears his call, stops,
and asks for Bartimaeus to come to him. When Bartimaeus is told that Jesus
will speak with him he springs up, throws off his cloak, and goes to stand
before Jesus. Jesus asks, "What do you want me to do for you?" Bartimaeus
responds, "My teacher, let me see again." Jesus tells him that his faith has
made him well, Bartimaeus' eyes are opened and he leaves all behind and follows Jesus out of the city.

If you were begging by the side of the road, what would be the position
of your body? Move your body into the position you feel would best reflect
Bartimaeus's experience. Pay attention to your hands and arms and the position of your head. Close your eyes to simulate blindness. Imagine you hear
the crowd approaching, and someone tells you it is Jesus. Feel the shout rising in your throat and call out, "Jesus, son of David, have mercy on me."
Feel what it is like to be silenced and to ignore the warning and to shout
again. When Jesus calls to you spring up, throw off your cloak and go to
him. Feel the hope of Bartimaeus in that swift movement. Imagine asking
Jesus for your sight, hearing him bless your faith, and opening your eyes.

What is the moment of healing like? Do you know in your body and soul why Bartimaeus left all he knew to follow Jesus?

When a story has more than one person in it, the relationship between the people can be explored, as well as the relationship of each person to Jesus. When Jesus visits Mary and Martha (Luke 10:38-42), Mary sits at his feet, listening to all that he is saying. Martha is in the kitchen preparing the meal for Jesus and his followers. Martha comes from the kitchen asking Jesus to tell her sister to help her with the work she has been doing alone. Jesus tells Martha that she is worried and distracted about many things and that Mary has chosen the better part and it will not be taken from her.

What might the experiences of these sisters teach you about your own spiritual life? With this story in mind, pretend you are Mary and place your body at the feet of the imagined Jesus. Listen to what he is saying to you. Feel in your body what it is like to be this close to Jesus, taking in all of his words. Imagine Martha coming into the room asking Jesus to tell you to help her in the kitchen. Hear her say: "Lord, do you not care that my sister has left me to do all the work by myself?" Hear Jesus say that you have chosen the better part and it will not be taken from you. Hear Jesus' words in your body. What might you wish to say to Martha?

Shake off the experience of Mary, and take on the body position of Martha. How would Martha hold her body as she came from the kitchen to confront Jesus and Mary? See Mary at the feet of Jesus and hear Jesus gently rebuke you. "Martha, Martha, you are worried and distracted by many things. . . . " Feel his words in your body. What would you like to say to Jesus? What would you like to say to Mary?

Some of the stories of Jesus may be the easiest passages to be read from the inside out because they involve so many people to whom we can relate. We can put ourselves physically into the biblical descriptions: standing up, moving forward, shouting, reaching out, kneeling, begging, praising God. In a slightly different way, our bodies can also help us respond to the Psalms and other poetry of the Hebrew scripture. When reading these passages we do not become characters; rather, we allow the words to touch our souls and we invite our bodies to express what we know.

Psalm 43 is a prayer to God in time of trouble. The prayer asks God for defense against the unjust, mourns the experience of oppression, and asks God for guidance. When God hears the pleas, the prayer turns into a hymn of gratitude and praise. As you read the psalm slowly, verse by verse, stop and let your body express the words. Remain seated and use your upper body—your arms and hands and head.

> Vindicate me, O God, and defend my cause
> against an ungodly people;

How would your body respond to these words? Do you raise your arms in supplication? Do you cross your arms over your breast in a posture of defense? Let your body be your guide through this beautiful prayer.

> from those who are deceitful and unjust
> deliver me!

Does your position change? Does one movement flow into another?

> For you are God in whom I take refuge;
> why have you cast me off?
> Why must I walk about mournfully
> because of the oppression of the enemy?

How does your body express grief? How does your body mourn?

> O send out your light and your truth;
> let them lead me;
> let them bring me to your holy hill
> and to your dwelling.

How does your body shift when God's light and truth are there to lead you?

> Then I will go to the altar of God,
> to God my exceeding joy;
> And I will praise you with the harp,
> O God, my God.

Where do you feel joy in your body? How might your arms and hands and head and face express this joy?

> Why are you cast down, O my soul,
> and why are you disquieted within me?
> Hope in God; for I shall again praise him,
> my help and my God.

How does your body end this prayer? How does it rest after pouring out its fear and grief, its relief and gratitude?

After you have read and moved this psalm once and you have experienced the awkwardness of trying something new, go back and read and move again. And then again, until the words and your body become one. If you worry what you look like, or whether your movements are right, or whether this way of reading the Bible is silly, remember that God is the focus of this reading, and prayer is what this movement is about. Deepening your relationship with God is the intent. Allow your body to move your soul toward God.

In addition to the book of Psalms, the poetry of the Hebrew prophets, the book of Lamentations, or the book of Job can be read and prayed this way. How might your body respond to the familiar words of Isaiah?

> The spirit of the Lord God is upon me,
>   because the Lord has anointed me;
> he has sent me to bring good news to the oppressed,
>   to bind up the brokenhearted,
> to proclaim liberty to the captives,
>   and release to the prisoners. (Isa. 61:1)

A final suggestion about allowing your body to guide your Bible study: Read aloud. When you read aloud you engage your ears as well as your eyes. Your lips move and you can feel the words in your throat and on your tongue. When you read aloud you are forced to slow down and savor the words and their message. If you are not alone when you are reading, and your voice would bother others, move your lips. The very simple movement of your lips may guide you into the holy writing in a new and wondrous way.

Befriending the Body

To recognize the wisdom in our bodies, to listen to the knowledge stored in our very cells, to allow our bodies to be our teachers, we must be in the right relationship with our physical selves. I said to a friend once: "What do you think of your body? Do you like it?" He replied: "It's the only one I've got." How true! And yet we don't always act that way. How many times have we wished our bodies to be different? When we are young we want to be older. When we are old we want to be younger. We may want to be thinner or stronger or faster or more graceful. We wish we were taller or shorter or prettier. We want our hair to be curlier, or straighter, or longer, or thicker. We want and we wish, but the body we have is the only one we have.

We often treat our bodies like beasts of burden rather than temples of God that have been loaned to us for safekeeping. We think about whipping our bodies into shape, or starving them into thinness, or pounding them into condition. Sometimes when our bodies need attention, we try to ignore them and treat them like pesky acquaintances. Other times we treat our bodies as if they are gods rather than temples of God. We lavish such love and attention on them that our bodies become the center of our lives. We become consumed by how we look. We take trips to the surgeon trying to improve on this gift of flesh we have been given by God.

Learning to pray with body and soul means finding a balanced approach to our embodiment. When we are balanced, we treat our bodies as intimate friends. In close friendship, we seek to know the other and at the same time honor the mystery of who the other is. In close friendship, conflict and stress will appear and disappear, giving the relationship a rhythm of its own. Sometimes we will take our friend for granted, at other times pour great love and energy into the friendship. We know that the friendship changes over time and that we risk stifling its beauty if we hold on too tight. Intimate friendship teaches us about loving and letting go, because we know that the other does not belong to us but has come into our life as a gift. In friendship we make a commitment to that gift.

A balanced relationship with our bodies has all these elements of friendship: love, letting go, conflict, change, commitment. We seek to know our bodies while we honor the mystery of our bodies. We attend to our bodies when they are in great need. We also attend when all is going well. We commit ourselves to care for our bodies. We thank God for the body that has been given, for it is the only one we have.

But this attitude of friendship, respect, care, and thanksgiving has not always been part of our Christian tradition. Although at the heart of Christianity is the belief that in Jesus Christ the divine became fully human, Christians have sometimes been unable to make a graceful link between the body of Jesus and the bodies of the rest of humanity.

Many attitudes toward the human body have been expressed throughout Christian history. At times attention to the body, to the language of the body, and to experiences of the body were absent from Christian writings. In these periods, the body was simply ignored. In other periods of history, the body was denied. At other times Christians were exhorted to control their bodies because bodily appetites and activities were viewed as a hindrance to spiritual development. Sometimes the followers of Jesus were taught to transcend their bodies in an attempt to live in the purely spiritual realm. Some Christians were taught to mortify the body, punishing themselves with whips, hair shirts, and beds of nails.

We would be wise not to overcompensate for centuries of misguided teachings about our bodies. "Body-centered spirituality" is a term frequently used to indicate a positive relationship with the body. I believe the intent of this phrase is to make sure that we know that the body is not excluded from the spiritual life. We are at risk of idolatry, however, if we place the body, rather than God, at the center of our spiritual lives. Paul says: "Glorify God in your body" (1 Cor. 6:20). He does not say: "Glorify your body." In a culture that idolizes the body, we need to be careful to find a balance between denial and idolatry, between mortification and glorification. We find this balance by embracing our bodies just as they are and taking them or following them into relationship with God.

Fasting

Fasting is the practice of giving up food for a period of time to make space in our lives to be more intentional about our relationship to God. To many people, fasting feels like an unfriendly way to treat our bodies. But when we fast with tenderness toward our bodies, with openness to lessons the body in fast can teach us, and with our hearts focused on God, we may discover new ways to be in prayer:

> "During my fast," a young man said, "I realized how much time I spend thinking about food. The hunger I felt was easy compared to the extra time I had which I had to decide what to do with."

> "The hunger I experienced was so minimal compared to the hunger of so many people in this world. I spent much of my day being grateful for the abundance with which I have been blessed, and offering prayers for those living in scarcity."

> "I became aware of how unconscious I am about food. Not eating sharpened my senses. I became aware of the variety of smells associated with food. I saw an apple that became beautiful before my eyes. When I broke my fast with a piece of bread, I felt like I was attending a feast."

Fasting has been part of Judeo-Christian prayer tradition since the time of Moses. People fasted in times of sorrow and defeat. David fasted when his child was ill and lay all night on the ground. "The elders of his house stood beside him, urging him to rise from the ground; but he would not, nor did he eat food with them" (2 Sam. 12:16-6). When the Israelites lost eighteen thousand armed men to the Benjamites, "The whole army went back to Bethel and wept, sitting there before the Lord; they fasted that day until evening (Judg. 20:26)."

Fasting was also a way to prepare for a coming event. Moses fasted forty days and forty nights as he received and wrote the Ten Commandments on Mount Sinai (Exod. 34:28). Jesus fasted forty days and forty nights in the wilderness in preparation for his ministry among us (Matt. 4:2).

Jesus gave no instructions about fasting, except to say that when we fast we are not to call attention to ourselves but rather "put oil on your head and wash your face, so that your fasting may be seen not by others but by your God who is in secret" (Matt. 6:17-8). In the early church, fasting occasionally became part of worship (Acts 13:2).

Today we most commonly hear of people making a public fast to draw attention to a cause. Fasting becomes the means to an end, the end being a change of policy, a change of direction, or a change of heart. We rarely hear of people who privately fast as part of their individual prayer practice, and yet fasting is another way our bodies can teach us about our relationship with God.

Reintroducing fasting is risky in a society that has so many problems with food. Eating disorders are rampant. Many people are in constant pursuit of the perfect meal. Some in our society are hooked on junk foods, while others are obsessed with health foods. Most teenage girls have been on a diet at some time in their lives. But fasting is truly not about food. Rather, fasting is about spaciousness. Through fasting we create a temporary emptiness in which we can find God.

In his book *Addiction and Grace*, Gerald May says that as much as we long for God, we seem to avoid a relationship with God by filling our time with other activities.[2] We want time with God, but we spend our time in other ways. Our activities may be good, helpful, creative, or productive, but they still may keep us from God. God is found (and God finds us) in the spacious moments of life when we are willing to cease our activities, to stop our relentless doing and simply be. Because we do not know how to "do" this, we are afraid. The spaciousness of pure being terrifies us. But we must learn to be with the emptiness if we are to meet God. Fasting gives us an experience of spaciousness. We might learn from our fast how to live with the emptiness and therefore begin to make more room in our lives and our hearts for God.

When we fast for a period of time, we create emptiness within our bodies and we create space in our lives. For the duration of our fast we do not need to concern ourselves with food in our usual ways. We do not have to plan our meals, we have no need to shop, there is no preparation, no time spent eating and no cleaning up. We create space inside and out, and for that day we learn to live in the emptiness. As we attend to the spaciousness, we are given the opportunity to pay attention to the ways we usually fill our lives. With this awareness we may discover new ways of filling our lives with God.

If you decide to fast, keep the purpose of your fast before you. Why are you fasting? What will you attend to? What do you have to learn? Be clear that fasting is *not* an exercise in weight loss. Neither is it a punishment of your body. By fasting we honor our bodies, recognizing them as our teachers.

The best schedule for a twenty-four hour fast is from noon to noon. Begin your fast after a light lunch. Drink plenty of water during your fast. Break your fast with fruit and rice or grains. During your fast be intentionally prayerful. Use the time to attend to the presence of God in your life. You may wish to journal, or read the Bible or sing. Begin and end your fast with a prayer. You might choose familiar prayers, seek out new prayers, or write your own prayer for this special occasion.

As you think about the practice of fasting and its possible place in your own life, reflect on the story told by Thomas Keating about the experience of a young monk, who eagerly looked forward to Lent one year. He was very excited about fasting. In his enthusiasm he began to imagine how he would be able to maintain his fast, how little food he would be able to get along on, and how he would most likely "out-fast" the other brothers. When the young monk described to his abbot his great desire for the purity he would achieve this Lent, the abbot listened kindly and then was silent. He was quiet and still for a long time and then he said: "Son, fasting is not about achievement. Fasting is not about pride. This Lent I wish you to eat your regular meals, and in addition at least one chocolate bar a day!"

There are some people who should not fast from food for physical or emotional reasons. If you think you are one of these people, listen to your body and soul and decide carefully. If the experience of fasting still appeals to you, you could fast from something other than food. Although fasting is usually associated with food, it truly means giving up, for a while, something we believe to be essential. You might fast from your TV or your sound system. You might fast from your car. You might give up listening to the news or reading the newspaper. Look to your own life to see what is habitual, what you seem to do almost unconsciously every day. Explore the possibilities of what you might do without. Remember that the purpose of fasting from anything is not punishment or even denial. The purpose of fasting is to create space in your life to attend to God.

Liturgical Movement

As we become more attuned to the messages our bodies send us, we can discover important information about community prayer and our liturgical practices. Have you experienced a difference in Holy Communion when you are served the elements in the pews or when you go forward to receive them at the altar? The bread and wine are the same. The words of institution are the same. But your body is involved differently. Your movements may evoke different responses and can profoundly affect your experience of the sacrament.

When we are served communion in the pews, our bodies are quiet, at rest, receptive. The minister serves elders or lay people who in turn serve the people. After being fed, the congregation is charged to go out in the world and serve all people. This way of distributing communion reenacts Jesus serving the disciples.

If we go forward to receive the bread and the cup, our bodies become active. We must stand, walk forward, lift our hands. Although we again receive, we have been called to stand up and seek out the gifts that await us. If we gather around the table to receive, as the disciples gathered around Jesus, we not only stand up for our beliefs, but we also place ourselves side by side with brothers and sisters in faith. In this circle, we acknowledge that we are each dependent upon the other as well as dependent upon God.[3]

Experiencing in our bodies different ways of reenacting the Lord's Supper helps us to know how to pray. As I sit quietly and wait, I may offer prayers of repentance, knowing the healing power of communion. As I stand and walk forward, I may find myself calling on God for courage. As I join my community around the table, I may be called to pray, for them and for all those who are not at the table, that they too may find in some way the healing power of God's love.

Learning new ways to pray through changing liturgical practices can be difficult. We all grow comfortable in the way things are. But when we are willing to learn from our bodies we become more willing to experiment, seeing new experiences as opportunities for learning how to pray.

When a young pastor decided one Sunday to have the congregation come forward to place their offerings on the altar instead of putting them in the baskets passed by the ushers most of the people complained. They did not like getting up and walking forward; they thought it took too long; they saw no point in the change. But one woman said later that as she held her money in her hand and walked slowly down the aisle, she began to realize that the money was just a symbol. As she walked she knew that she was placing herself on the altar; she was giving herself to God. "When I sit in my place and the basket comes around, I feel like the church is *taking* my money from me and that my offering has nothing to do with God," she exclaimed. Without the opportunity to walk forward this woman may never have received her insight, an insight that led her to reexamine her relationship with God.

Liturgical Dance

Most of us will never be liturgical dancers, but many of us will experience liturgical dance as part of a worship experience. When we watch a liturgical dancer, our own bodies can become involved even though we are not dancing and probably not moving at all. If we are open to the experience something happens in our own bodies when we witness the movements of another. When we watch a child skip, we may feel our hearts skip even if our bodies stay still. If we see a fight break out, each blow might feel as if we are the ones being struck. As we watch a dancer or a group of dancers move to the words of a favorite hymn, or take the positions of a familiar Bible story, or dance the stories of our faith, we can experience through their bodies a new level of understanding.

One Good Friday, soon after I had lost a close friend to AIDS, I attended a service during which a group of dancers reenacted the crucifixion of Jesus. They moved with grace and solemn dignity from Pilate's proclamation of death to the ridicule from the crowds to the physical struggle of carrying the cross, through the nailing and the mocking and the tortuous wait for death. Watching them dance I felt this familiar story in my body and soul. Yet all the hearings, all the readings did not prepare me for the felt experience. When the dancers took Jesus from the cross and carried him out, the tears were streaming down my face and my whole body was shaking. I was there at the foot of the cross as I had been at the bedside of my friend. The enormity of death opened up before me and I discovered layer upon layer of new meaning in the familiar Good Friday event.

Carla De Sola, a liturgical dancer writes:

> Breathing, the dancer moves
> Spirit gently bonding with her soul
>   dancing with bone and breath.
> Her soul, infused with spirit
>   is shaping her body, and her body, her soul.
> Body and soul become as one,
>   living moving being.[4]

If we are willing to open our hearts to the dancer's experience, *our* souls are infused with the spirit, and *our* bodies and souls become one. When this happens, we need not pray, because we have *become* prayer, and we have not moved a muscle.

ACTIVITIES FOR REFLECTION AND DISCUSSION

1. Remember and reflect on the ways you were taught to pray. Were you taught at home, in church, in school? Who taught you to pray? What were the messages about your body in relation to prayer? Make a list of the teachings you wish to retain in your adult practice of prayer. Make a list of those teachings you realize no longer have meaning for you. Discuss your memories and your insights with a friend or in your book group.

2. The idea of resting in God is one that appeals to many of us in our busy world, but we do not know how to stop long enough to discover a prayer of rest. Our bodies can teach us our own personal way to pray and

rest in God. In the privacy of your own home, quiet your body and mind and imagine yourself resting in God. What physical position best reflects this prayer? Is it sitting comfortably in a large chair wrapped in a blanket? Is it curled up on your bed with your arms wrapped around a pillow? Is it flat on your back on the floor or outside under the sky? Let your imagination roam, and allow your body to take on different positions until you have found your own unique prayer of rest. Practice resting in God for a brief time every day, and reflect on how this practice affects your relationship with God.

3. To enter into an experience of forgiveness with body and soul, turn to Luke 7:36-50, the story of a sinful woman who goes to Jesus for forgiveness. Using your imagination and physical movements, act out the journey of the woman as she goes to the Pharisee's house where Jesus is eating. Envision yourself going into the house where you were not invited and where you would not be welcome. Stand behind the imaginary Jesus with a jar of ointment. Kneel down and imagine weeping and washing Jesus' feet with your tears and drying them with your hair. Allow your body to move through this process of washing, drying, kissing, and anointing. Then imagine hearing Jesus' words: "Your sins are forgiven. . . . Your faith has saved you; go in peace." Feel those words in your body and soul, then rise, and walk out the door, freed of whatever burden you were carrying when you arrived. Write a brief prayer of gratitude for the healing that accompanies the forgiveness of sins.

Other Bible stories that invite being read and prayed with body and soul are:

> The wise and foolish bridesmaids (Matt. 25:1-13)
> The watchful doorkeeper (Mark 13:34-36)
> The good Samaritan (Luke 10:30-37)
> The friend at midnight (Luke 11:5-8)
> The lost coin (Luke 15:8-10)
> A woman's hemorrhage cured (Matt. 9:20-22)

4. When we prayed Psalm 43 with our bodies, we were deepening our individual relationship to God. We can also use our bodies to pray this or any psalm as a group. Allow the members of a group to get the feel of the psalm in their bodies as was described in this chapter. When people are ready and willing, have someone volunteer for the first part of the first verse. As the narrator reads the words, the pray-er allows his or her body to take the position that reflects those words. Then, instead of moving the body into the next verse, the pray-er holds the position for the length of the psalm. A second pray-er who is standing next to the first pray-er finds a physical form for the second verse and holds that position. Then a third pray-er does the next part

of the following verse and so on until the whole psalm has been sculpted by the pray-ers in the group. This activity is as powerful for the ones who see the psalm take shape as it is for the ones who move and hold the various verses of the psalm. The physical depiction of a psalm is an excellent prayer activity to be practiced by youth, and it is a wonderful experience for the congregation who witnesses the prayer.

2

OUR SENSUALITY AND SEXUALITY HELP US KNOW GOD

Young children learn through their bodies. They listen for sounds, delighting in the familiar, startling at the unexpected, curious about all that is around them. Their eyes are bright as they take in wondrous sights. If something interests them, they stare and stare and stare. Children will put anything and everything into their mouths. They follow their noses to all sorts of smells. Children touch not only with their hands; they use their whole bodies to feel—rolling in the grass, running barefoot in the sand, throwing their arms around you. Children take all of God's creation in through their senses, not only learning about the world but also coming to know God. Children live a sensuous theology.

We adults would be wise to follow the children. Instead, we *think* about God, building abstractions in our heads. We *argue* about images of God, trying to discover the best way to address God. We *worry* about sin and salvation, about God's anger and love, whether God is all-powerful, or all love, or all of everything. These are important concerns for people of faith, because we long to know God. But we limit our knowledge if we depend only on our heads.

Knowing God

In classes devoted to expanding our understanding of prayer I ask participants to fill in the following blanks with words that come from their own experience:

I know God when I see _____.
I know God when I hear _____.
I know God when I touch _____.
I know God when I taste _____.
I know God when I smell _____.

People often begin their thinking by filling in the blanks with experiences related to the church: seeing the cross or the stained glass windows; hearing hymns or church bells; touching the rosary; tasting communion wine or juice and the bread of life; smelling incense. But others jump right in with experiences from their everyday lives. We may know God when we see a sunrise, the smile of a child, a beautiful painting, or a budding flower. We may know God when we hear the cry of a gull, a symphony, or the whistle of a person at work. We may know God when we touch a seashell, or hold a puppy, or feel the sun gently warming our backs. We may know God when we taste the tears of a loved one, drink cold water on a hot day, or let rich chocolate melt in our mouths. We may know God when we smell fresh bread, pine trees, the scent of our lover, or newly mowed hay.

When we realize how many ways there are to know God, we may be startled by how close God is, and how easily known. With God so close, our hearts are stirred, and we know our love for God in new and wondrous ways. Our love for God, for others, and for creation become one. Jürgen Moltman expressed it this way:

> When I love God, I love the beauty of bodies, the rhythm of movements, the shining of eyes, the embraces, the feelings, the scents, the sounds of all this protean creation. When I love you, my God, I want to embrace it all, for I love you with all my senses in the creations of your love. In all the things that encounter me, you are waiting for me.[1]

With God so close, so immediate, prayer becomes easy, for our response to God is sensual and natural. We simply shift our attention and see God revealed in what and whom we are hearing and tasting and holding and seeing and smelling and loving.

One summer I was hiking alone on the Colorado Trail. The sky was clear and brilliantly blue, the breeze was soft with the scent of pine. I saw small animals and occasionally heard the call of birds. The water I carried was refreshing and the sandwich nourishing. I felt very blessed to be alive and walking through this beautiful world. All of a sudden I heard a voice within my head: "You should be praying!" I was brought up short. I was confused.

"Do I stop and bow my head?" I wondered. "Do I fall to my knees?" And then I understood. My new awarenesses of God's constant presence allowed me to hear the inner admonition not as a command to fall to my knees but as a call simply to pay attention. The voice was really saying: "Pay attention to God in all that you are experiencing." I breathed in the spirit of God. I breathed out my gratitude. I knew I was praying. I knew I was a prayer.

Intention and Attention

When I tell these stories and encourage people to discover God through their senses, to attend to God in every moment, to love God in our loving of creation, a question arises: "Does this mean that *everything* is prayer?"

Everything can *become* prayer. Turning our very lives into prayer takes our intention and our attention. Our intention is why we do something, the purpose of our activity. I may walk to stay healthy, read the Bible because someone suggested it. I may fix my stepson's lunch to help him get ready for school, listen to music to relax. There are wise and wonderful reasons for doing many of the things we do. We act out of love or from responsibility or for self-care. These activities in themselves are not prayer, but they can become prayer. Our daily actions can become prayer in two ways.

One way is to consciously shift our intention. I may decide to walk for the purpose of opening all my senses to God's presence around me. I may read the Bible out loud, chewing on the words, discovering God in the text. I may make the school lunch for the purpose of knowing God more deeply through my loving relationship with my child. Or I may listen for God in the music. Activities can become prayers if we approach the activity with the intent of knowing God more fully and loving God more deeply.

When my mother turned eighty and her arthritis was getting worse, she was finding it hard to do the walking the doctor told her she needed. She confessed to me one day that she just wasn't walking, even though she knew she should and had even found a place to walk which had a railing and felt safe. "Every morning I think, 'Today I will walk!' and then I don't," she said. "I guess I see no point in trying to strengthen this tired old decrepit body."

I had just finished reading *A Guide to Walking Meditation* by the Buddhist monk Thich Nhat Hanh.[2] He describes the practice of walking and breathing and opening your heart to the experience of the moment. He writes of the value of walking slowly with no destination in mind. He suggests images and phrases to help you focus your attention:

> "Please try visualizing a lotus flower opening as your feet touch the ground. . . . "
> "Walk so that your footprints bear only the marks of peaceful joy and complete freedom."
> "Place your foot on the surface of the earth the way an emperor would place his seal on a royal decree."
> "Each step will cause a breeze to rise."

Although Thich Nhat Hanh writes from a Buddhist perspective — and my mother was a Christian — I thought this beautiful book might be helpful to her, so I sent her a copy with a note of encouragement. She had no trouble finding in the Eastern wisdom truth consistent with her own faith, because the next week she called in great excitement. "I'm walking!" she exclaimed. "I'm walking! It feels like I'm walking with God."

Another way an activity becomes prayer is when God shifts our intention by grabbing our attention. We are walking along, hurrying to get somewhere, thinking of all the things we need to do and we spy an early bloom pushing up from the wet earth at the edge of snow. We are reading a novel and a certain description or turn of phrase touches a memory and turns our attention to God.

When I am consumed with worry about my teenager and he walks into the room and says blithely, "Love ya, Jane," dropping a kiss in the vicinity of my cheek, I am filled with gratitude. When I am driving a familiar route and a dog darts out in front of me I swerve, missing the animal and avoiding a collision with an oncoming car. I am left shaken at encountering so suddenly the fragility of life, and I breathe a prayer of thanksgiving for my safety and the safety of others.

All these examples of discovering God with our senses are pleasurable experiences — moments that bring us joy or gratitude, awe or release. We are reminded of God through activities and people we love. God grabs our attention with the wonder of creation, a moment of safety. But what are we to do when we encounter the pain and the brokenness and the ugliness of life?

When I was in seminary, I took a class titled "Styles of Christian Prayer." One of the first activities offered was the practice of moving through the world with the instruction to encounter anything and everything in our daily lives with the words, "This too speaks of God." As we practiced, we ran into difficulty. How did the litter speak of God? How did the angry voices from next door speak of God? How did the headlines of corruption and terror and oppression speak of God?

When we returned to class the following week, one class participant was angry. "You are turning our attention only to the good and the beautiful when you ask us to look at things and say: 'This too speaks of God.' What about injustice? What about brokenness? As Christians we are not to turn away. We are to address these issues, to find justice, to console. There is too much Pollyanna in all this, if you ask me!"

The instructor was silent for a moment before he responded: "I am not asking you to turn away. Oh no! I am challenging all of us to confront these difficult issues of life. But I am inviting you to see them with the eyes and the heart of God. Litter speaks of God, for it reminds us of the need for individuals and society to care for God's creation. Angry people speak of God, for they remind us of the need for reconciliation. Oppression and terror remind us of the words of the prophet Amos:

> Let justice roll down like waters,
> and righteousness like an ever flowing stream.
> (Amos 5:24)

All of life reminds us that God is with us. The good and the beautiful and the loving illuminate God's love and promise. The broken and the ugly remind us of the 'not yet' of God's promise. When we open our hearts to the 'not yet' we find new ways to pray."

A lively class discussion followed. "What is your prayer when you hear the sirens of an ambulance?" "Is it possible to read the news prayerfully?" "How do you pray when your children fight?" We discovered together an amazing range of prayers and prayer practices. We learned to turn our attention to God by encountering life with all of our senses. Whether we experienced pleasure or discomfort, joy, or disgust, we could find God in our midst. All of life became an invitation to deepen our relationship with God.

Sensual Prayers

Early childhood experiences in nature can remind us of how fully sensual prayers can be. When we are young, often before we have been "taught" to pray, we are praying regularly with all of who we are. Adults in our lives may not have recognized those activities as prayer, and if we look back using a narrow lens to look at prayer we may also miss our early experiences of God. But with our eyes and hearts expanded through the discussion of knowing God with our senses we may find many prayers in our memories.

A house painter remembered a childhood prayer that simply grew out of his young being. He would run outside early in the morning and spin around on the grass with his arms thrown wide, shouting, "Hello God! Here I am!" He reported, "When I learned prayers from memory and was taught about praying in church, I discounted that childhood experience and was even embarrassed to recall it."

A nurse recalled climbing high into a tree, sitting silently, and seeing her family and neighbors and strangers passing by on the street. She watched and she listened and she thought, "I wonder if this is how God watches and listens to us."

When I was asked to remember an early experience of prayer in a guided meditation, an early memory came back to me immediately, vividly, and in great detail:

> I was nine years old, on vacation with my parents in the Sierra Nevada mountains. One morning we set out on a day hike over soft trails that wound through meadows, along streams, and into shadowy woods. We

stopped at noon for a picnic lunch, after which my parents stretched out
in quiet contentment, and I set off to explore the surrounding area. I
clambered up a wonderfully smooth granite boulder and settled myself in
a natural seat I discovered on the other side. The wind was soft on my
face, the sun warm on my back. As I sat, I noticed a trail of the largest
ants I had ever seen walking by my left foot. I watched in fascination as
they marched by seemingly intent on their destination. I idly wondered
what it would be like to step on one, and then, without much thought, I
lifted my little red tennis shoe and ended the life of one ant. As I heard
the crunch of death, I was overcome by what I had done. I was ashamed
and scared. Lifting my face upward I breathed, "Oh my God!"

I remember returning to my parents and trying to tell them what had
happened, but I imagine I did not make much sense. I remember talking
about the sun and the wind, the ants and their march to somewhere. I
remember mumbling about what that one ant experienced as this huge
foot came out of the sky, and what if, what if God were a big foot in the
sky, and my life . . . That was as far as I got, for my mother heard my fear
and rushed to reassure me. "God is love," my mother said. "God wishes
you no harm." My father also heard my fear but took another way to
comfort me. "You know all about the sun and the planets and how they
move. A big foot in the sky is not logical."

I remember being comforted but realized that my parents did not
understand. Neither did I. I knew something important had happened
but I did not know what. I had no words. It never occurred to me that I
was in prayer. Prayers were words you recited, I thought. Prayers were
what you did in church or at meals or at bedtime. Prayers were boring
and incomprehensible words from the minister. Prayers happened in the
company of others, not alone, unplanned, atop a granite boulder. So I
relaxed into my parents' presence and accepted the ritual chocolate bar
before we started hiking. I let the experience and all the accompanying
feelings fade.

Our early experiences of prayer are often discounted because they are
so unique and personal that they fit no accepted form of prayer. Usually
these experiences come as a surprise, breaking in on us and leaving us gasp-
ing. Even as we become adults we often discount prayerful experiences if
they do not fit some recognized form. An elderly farmer told me he only
prayed in church. He never prayed at home. "Oh, no," he mused. "When I'm
on the land I don't pray. I simply walk and talk and breathe with God."

As adults we can honor and celebrate the natural ways we prayed as
children. We can also discover natural and sensual ways to pray in this
period of our lives. Although we may not climb a tree to discover God's view
of the world, or spin into the early morning sunshine shouting out to God,
we could wrap ourselves in a warm blanket and go outside in the middle of

the night to look at the stars and wonder at the mystery of creation. Sometime we could find ourselves caught in a warm spring rain and, instead of running for cover, we could stop and spread our arms out and tilt our faces upward and receive God's blessing through our very pores. We could sit by the ocean listening to the sounds of the waves, feeling the rhythms as the pulse of the universe, knowing the pulse to be the heartbeat of God. We could gaze at the lofty mountains in the distance and imagine the mountains gazing back at us.

The natural world is filled with opportunities for prayer. All we need to do is open our senses to the wonder that surrounds us. However we respond to that wonder—with awe, delight, fear, or gratitude—we are in prayer, because we are responding to God's call to relationship.

Musical Prayers

We do not need to be in nature to pray naturally and sensually. Whether we listen to music or make music, individually or in a group, our experience can be both sensual and prayerful. Hymns are often held in our memories long after Bible verses, sermon statements, or spoken prayers have faded. Although I rarely sing on key, I love to raise my voice in hymns or chants or prayers set to music. Certain hymns always make me weep, while others bring forth a sense of joy and delight. Using my voice is a sensual and emotional experience because I can feel the vibrations and taste the notes as well as hear the melody. Hildegard of Bingen, eleventh-century mystic and musician, wrote about the human voice:

> The body is truly the garment of the soul, which has a living voice, for that reason it is fitting that the body simultaneously with the soul repeatedly sing praises to God through voice.[3]

A friend of mine who sings in a small a capella group described an experience of voice unlike any other she had ever had:

> We were preparing some lovely choral music for Christmas, and had the opportunity to practice in a room that had perfect acoustics. As an experiment, we decided to stand in a circle facing each other and sing one of our pieces as softly as we could, trying to match vowel sounds and breathing and pitch exactly. It took us a few minutes to match each other with the exactness we were aiming for, but after a while we got it, and the effect was extraordinary. It was as though the sound suddenly became a single voice, even though we were singing five-part harmony. The totality of that sound blended with the resonance of the room. The energy of that sound, quiet as it was, seemed to lift the singers. It felt as though we were floating slightly off the floor.[4]

Our music listening and music making does not need to be in church or be religious to become a prayer. Music and nature combine when we make music outside or hear tones, melodies, and rhythms of the natural world. Once I was walking across a meadow, listening to the natural sounds, when suddenly I also heard a flute echoing and responding to the insects and the birds and the wind. A young man was sitting on a boulder playing his silver flute with his eyes closed and his very being a part of the music and the world around him. I stopped to listen for a while then walked on quietly, leaving him to his solitary prayer.

When we use our intention to place God at the center of our lives, musical opportunities are all around us. A woman told me, with shy embarrassment, that she liked to listen to love songs. "I listen and sing along and hear the words as a love song between me and God. This is a wonderful way for me to be in prayer." A man told me in the middle of a silent retreat that he deeply regretted not bringing his guitar. "I thought we were going to 'make no noise' and that a musical instrument would be out of place. But so much is happening within me as I draw closer to God. My prayer is coming in the form of music and I have no way to let it out."

We don't have to be musical to have music become a form of prayer. We don't have to play an instrument or sing or even know much about music. But we know what we enjoy listening to, we know what draws us into relationship with God. We can seek out that music and listen with our hearts attuned to God. Listening to music of all forms can be a way of listening to God.

Praying by Hand

Touch is a wonderful sense. Think of walking barefoot in warm sand or on grass wet with morning dew. Remember what it feels like to have a baby grab your finger, or to have a friend gently massage your shoulders and neck. Have you ever slipped into warm flannel on a cold night, or placed silk directly against your skin? Imagine touching the face of someone you love, or holding a smooth, water-worn rock in your hand, or caressing the leather binding of a favorite book. Touch is a vital part of relationship—with others, with ourselves, and with God.

Fingering prayer beads is a traditional prayer of touch. Prayer beads have been part of devotion in most religions over time and around the world. The beads may be used in a variety of ways such as counting mantras, or reciting the name of God, or pondering the mysteries of the gospel. Beneath the differences of the way the prayer beads are used is the common experience that fingering the beads aids concentration. Basil Pennington explains:

"While the beads occupy and integrate our external senses into our prayer, our mind is left freer to attend to its own level of reality. There are mysteries to be pondered and experiences to be had, moments of enlightenment and touches of the divine, while the beads and their accompanying formulas keep the lower faculties occupied."[5]

Christine Lore Weber, Catholic writer, teacher, and counselor, speaks of her own return to praying the rosary. "The rosary is a bodily prayer, a prayer of touch," she says. "Our hearts touch God when our fingers touch the beads."[6] Many Protestants are also discovering the rosary and integrating it into their own prayer life. Some use beads during intercessory prayer, naming a person each time they finger a bead. Other pray-ers who have begun to practice the prayer of the heart have bought or made their own string of prayer beads to keep count of the prayers they are repeating. Prayer beads of some kind may encourage you to recognize the constant presence of God in your life.

There are also less traditional ways of praying by hand. A student in a class on prayer turned in her reflections in the form of piecework and quilting. When asked to read a Bible passage and allow it to lead her into prayer, she would engage her mind, her imagination, her emotions and her body to get inside the story. She would sit quietly allowing images to form in her mind. Taking fabrics of different colors and textures she would arrange them to give form to her reflections and sew them together with a variety of stitches and colors of thread. When I received her work, I knew that I had been handed a prayer.

Even when it is not a class assignment, handwork is often a form of prayer. Building models, knitting and stitchery, painting, baking bread, throwing pots, weaving—all can become a form of prayer. I have a vivid memory of the scene from the movie *Gandhi*, in which Gandhi removes himself from the tumultuous activities in his quest for justice and sits in solitude spinning his own cotton.

The activity of our hands may free our minds and our hearts for God. But I also believe that the activity of our hands can become our actual prayer. We, in the image of God, can bring form out of chaos, order out of disorder, and give shape to our dreams of creation. With our intention and attention on God, our hands that build and sew and knead and paint and weave can imitate and embody the creative spirit of God.

One final idea for praying by hand—learn sign language. Most of us will not become fluent, but we can learn to sign familiar prayers and favorite hymns. We could learn to sign the prayer of the heart. We could learn the signs for God, for spirit, for prayer or for any other words that remind us of our commitment to our relationship with God. When we have learned our most important signs, we can teach them to others. Teaching the signs often builds a spiritual relationship between people and may introduce others to the wondrous possibility of praying by hand.

Sexuality and Spirituality

Knowing God through our senses, weaving a sensuous theology, and practicing sensual prayers, we acknowledge and celebrate our embodiment and our sensuality. To know and honor ourselves as sensual beings pushes us to know the fullness of ourselves as sexual beings. This fullness invites us to explore the connection between our sexuality and spirituality. If we know God through our sensuality, maybe we also know God through our sexuality.

Although the connection between sexuality and spirituality makes some uncomfortable, I have found that more people are both pleased and relieved to hear both subjects talked about in the same place. We may not be used to speaking about sexuality in church or about spirituality in the bedroom. But most people, if they are honest with themselves, know from experience that sexuality and spirituality belong together. They might even identify with the young student who rushed out of class after this material was presented, exclaiming to a friend: "I can't believe it! It's wonderful! We are actually talking about sex in prayer class!"

Another student had a more subdued response. She made an appointment with me for the next day, saying something had come up in class that she wished to speak to me about. When she arrived at my office, she was hesitant and seemed unsure of what she wanted to say. Finally she blurted out: "I've never told anyone this before."

She then proceeded to tell me about a profound mystical experience she had had almost ten years before. She had been at a mountain retreat site and had been in prayer for two days. She read the Bible. She found private places to sing. She walked and walked, and sat in nature feeling God all around her. One day she lay on a warm rock in the sun, with all her senses attuned. "Gradually I became aware that God was not only around me but within me. With this awareness came strong sexual feelings. I loved the experience of God within, but I was terrified of the bodily sensations. And I was so ashamed! I felt that my time of prayer and closeness with God had been ruined by my sexual experience. I decided I was doing something wrong. So I closed down my senses and my body to God and approached prayer purely from my mind." She was weeping quietly as she finished the story and we sat quietly together.

"Hearing the discussion of sexuality and spirituality yesterday amazed me," she said. "I listened from the context of my own experience, and what you were saying made sense. I can reclaim that experience now, not only as normal, but as a grace from God."

This woman was experiencing the fullness of her sexuality that we call *eros*.

> Eros is our passionate drive for life and growth. This meaning of erotic experience includes much more than genital arousal. Eros moves in all our longings to make contact, to be—quite literally—*in touch*. Arousal and affection, passion and response, intimacy and appreciation—these are all parts of eros. In erotic experience we first feel the connections between presence and pleasure, between longing and new life.[7]

With this description of eros we can see that sexuality is more than genital sex and sexual gratification. We can begin to understand that we are all sexual throughout our entire lives—old and young, sick or well, single or coupled, celibate or sexually active. In the words of James Nelson, "[Our] sexuality is the Creator's way of calling us out of separation, self-centeredness, and loneliness into communication and communion."[8]

Words of Caution

Celebrating our sexuality, discovering the deep connections between sexuality and spirituality, and allowing our sexuality to lead us into a new understanding of intimacy with God does not mean that all sexual thoughts lead us to God or that all sexual experiences are sacred. Sometimes during prayer we are distracted by sexual thoughts and fantasies that take our focus away from God. Usually these fantasies involve someone or something other than God, rather than the erotic experience of being loved totally by God.

If we are not careful, misplaced sexual fantasies can lead to sexual use or misuse of another. Sexual abuse is *never* an authentic spiritual experience. The misuse of another for our own release is *never* an image or echo of God's love for us. God's love is unconditional and invites mutuality, deep intimacy, and trust. The sexual abuse of another by a person in spiritual leadership is a sin. It is also a crime. When I hear of such events, I am able to understand why Christian history has tried to divide sexuality and spirituality. I believe that the church fathers may have experienced or foreseen the problems that could occur.

However, denial of our sexuality does not protect us from sin. Rather, knowing ourselves as sexual beings, and honoring and celebrating our sexuality while at the same time recognizing the possibility of danger, keeps us honest and faithful. The story of a mature woman in the role of retreat leader helps us understand how this process works:

During a long and profoundly moving retreat, I met with one of the retreatants to discuss his experiences of God and the meaning these experiences had for his life. He spoke about how his heart had been opened, about the gratitude he felt, about the possibilities he now saw in his life. As he was leaving our meeting, he expressed his gratitude to me. He quickly reached out for a hug and said, "I love you." His closeness and his words stirred something in me and I realized his lips were only inches away. I was filled with a moment of desire, but turned my head away from him, released the hug, and quietly said good-bye. As the door closed, I was shaken to my toes by what had almost happened. I knew his words and his actions came from his deep relationship with God and had little to do with me. But I was so touched by the passion in this man that I had almost lost my way. If I had turned my head toward him rather than away . . . I could hardly think of the consequences.

I was filled simultaneously with shame at what had almost happened and relief that it had not happened. Although I was embarrassed, I knew I needed to talk with my spiritual director about the incident. I needed to understand the dynamics of the situation to make sure that if such a thing happened again, I would be more prepared. I found great comfort in telling the story. My director helped me know that there was nothing shameful about my feelings. I had simply responded to what was happening in this retreatant's soul, but I would have broken a sacred covenant and committed a crime if I had acted on my momentary desire. Together we prayed in gratitude for the guidance I had received that kept me from sinning against this innocent man.

Biblical and Mystical Writings

Think for a moment of the words that you or others might use to describe a profound sexual experience with a committed loving partner. Words that are frequently used are *ecstasy, surrender, intimacy, vulnerability, joy, union, safety, and timeless and boundless love.* Now think of your relationship with God and a time of prayer that moved you deeply, an experience when you knew that you and God were one. What words describe this experience? Many of the same ones! In our deepest experiences of prayer, we find union and intimacy. Sometimes ecstasy and peace. We know the vulnerability of total surrender. We discover total acceptance and unconditional love.

This experience of passionate love is the theme of the Song of Songs, sometimes called the Song of Solomon, which is an erotic love poem in the middle of the Bible. The verses are filled with images of longing, intimacy, surrender, passion, and delight.

I slept, but my heart was awake.
Listen! My beloved is knocking.
"Open to me, my sister, my love,
  my dove, my perfect one;
for my head is wet with dew,
  my locks with the drops of the night." (5:2)

My beloved is all radiant and ruddy,
  distinguished among ten thousand.
His legs are alabaster columns,
  set upon bases of gold.
His appearance is like Lebanon,
  choice as the cedars.
His speech is most sweet,
  and he is altogether desirable
This is my beloved and this is my friend,
  O daughters of Jerusalem (5:10, 15-16)

You might wish to read the Song of Songs in its entirety. If you do, try reading it slowly, reading it aloud, reading it more than once. Listen for the affirmation of the goodness of our sexuality.

This poem celebrating human love and passion and sexual desire was read by the Jewish fathers as the story of God's love for Israel. The Christian church fathers "regarded the entire book as an allegory about the love between God and the human soul."[9] More recent interpretations of the Song of Songs have not disregarded the symbolic nature of the poem, but realize that "the ancient poem can symbolize God's passionate love for us only because erotic love is, itself, good and holy."[10]

From a Nazi prison camp, Lutheran pastor Dietrich Bonhoeffer wrote in praise of this beautiful poem:

> Even in the Bible we have the Song of Songs; and really one can imagine no more ardent, passionate, sensual love than is portrayed there. It's a good thing that the book is in the Bible, in face of all those who believe that the restraint of passion is Christian.[11]

The mystics also acknowledged the connection between sexuality and spirituality. The Christian mystical tradition tells of the union of the soul with God. In descriptions of this union, the language is filled with passion, ecstasy, and surrender. St. Therese of Lisieux has been called the Great Lover and in her poetry has expressed a lyric passion for her God.[12] In her poem "The Eternal Hymn, Sung from Exile," she wrote:

1. Your bride, who's exiled here
   upon this foreign shore,
Can yet sing hymns of love,
   eternal her desire,
For, O my Jesus! as
   in Heav'n for evermore,
So here on earth Your Love
   enflames her with its Fire!

4. Oh Love—I'm ablaze—
This soul be Your place!
Come here, of Your grace,
Come here, *consume me*.[13]

St. John of the Cross believed the soul of both women and men to be feminine; therefore he understood the soul to be the bride, and Christ the bridegroom. In "The Spiritual Canticle," first the bridegroom speaks, and then the bride:

22. The bride has entered
The sweet garden of her desire,
And she rests in delight,
Laying her neck
On the gentle arms of her Beloved.

27. There He gave me His breast;
There He taught me a sweet and living knowledge;
And I gave myself to Him,
Keeping nothing back;
There I promised to be His bride.[14]

In *The Dark Night of the Soul,* St. John of the Cross wrote poetically of the soul's surrender:

5. O guiding night!
O night more lovely than the dawn!
O night that has united
The lover and his beloved,
Transforming the beloved in her lover.

6. Upon my flowering breast
Which I kept wholly for him alone,
There he lay sleeping,
And I caressing him
There in a breeze from the fanning cedars.

7. When the breeze blew from the turret
Parting his hair,
He wounded my neck
With his gentle hand,
Suspending all my senses.

8. I abandoned and forgot myself,
Laying my face on my Beloved,
All things ceased: I went out from myself,
Leaving my cares
Forgotten among the lilies.[15]

Mystical language is sometimes sexual language. The Christian mystic "is driven to talk about the most intimate experiences of the spiritual life in the same words that are used to describe the most intimate experience of the earthly life, which is sexual union."[16]

Union as Grace

Although the mystics spoke of seeking union with God, I believe union with God comes as a gift, often when we least expect it. Simone Weil affirms this view when she writes, "Prayer is attention without aim." Another way of saying that is, "We attend to God simply to attend to God." We do not attend to God to find peace, or to experience ecstasy, to become holy, or to reach union. We pray simply to pray.

Doing something without a goal is not our way! Almost everything we do is to get somewhere else. We go to school to get a better job. We exercise to lower our blood pressure. We go to the movies to relax. We save our money for retirement or to leave to our children. Goal-oriented behavior is not wrong; in fact, it often serves us well. But goal orientation is not the way of prayer. Goals shift our attention from God to some expected result.

A delightful story tells of a medieval monk who was so filled with the spirit of God that every time he heard the name of Jesus, he would levitate. His long life of prayer and devotion to God had this surprising result, and he simply accepted it as a grace from God. But word began to spread across the countryside, and people came from all around to see this amazing monk. They would find him on the monastery grounds and say: "The peace of the Lord Jesus Christ be with you!" and the monk would slowly rise into the air. Soon people were asking him to teach them how to do that; they wanted to levitate too. The abbot understood that the people were being distracted from God by the monk's gift of levitation. He called the monk to him and said: "The fruit of your life of devotion has become the goal to many, so from now on, when you hear the name of Jesus, hold on!"

In the story, the monk's levitation was a grace from God but a distraction to his neighbors. Union with God is a grace, but, if we pursue the experience of union with God, it can become a distraction. We begin to seek the experiences we believe will accompany a mystical union. We shift our attention away from God. We are no longer praying without aim. We are no longer praying to pray. "Praying without aim" may be easier for us to understand if we think about our human relationships:

Jesus commanded his disciples to "love one another as I have loved you" (John 15:12). And so he commanded us. To love as Jesus loved is to love without aim. We do not love another so we will be secure. We do not love another to be loved in return. We do not love another to receive sexual gratification. We love to love. Sexuality and spirituality are both about relationship. As the soul longs for God, the soul longs for human companionship. In this longing, we reach out, we receive, we commit. Union with God or union with another may result from our longing. Ecstasy, joy, and peace may be gifts we receive. But we do not pursue gratification or union or ecstasy. In all relationships, human and divine, in prayer and in physical contact, we simply attend with love. We pray to pray. We love to love. And we wait for God's grace to find us.

ACTIVITIES FOR REFLECTION AND DISCUSSION

1. Sit quietly in the place in which you are reading this book. Take a moment to look around you at familiar objects, noticing colors and shapes and details. Then close your eyes and listen to the noises in your space. Do you hear traffic, other people, radios? Listen for the sounds and the silences. Become aware of the temperature in the room. Are you hot or cold or just right? Feel your body as it sits, or reclines, or lies down. Reach out your hand and touch the different textures of fabric, of furniture, or of objects close at hand. Then sniff for smells. Are there any? Are they familiar, pleasant, unpleasant? Do they evoke memories? If there is food or drink nearby, taste it intentionally—feel the full experience of swallowing. As you experience your surroundings with all your senses, reflect on how opening your senses could guide you in your relationship to God. Reflect on how your prayer life might expand if you were to open your senses more regularly and more fully to God. If these thoughts intrigue you, you might follow these sensual directions in your yard, in your neighborhood, at your place of work, or anywhere in your world.

2. Think for a moment about the many things you do with your hands. Perhaps you sit regularly at the computer fingering the keyboard. Maybe you are the one who folds laundry, weeds the garden, or waters the indoor plants. Maybe you have a hobby that requires use of your hands, or a young child whom you tend. Ask yourself how these activities could become prayers, so that you might experience praying by hand on a daily basis.

3. Find the Song of Songs in your Bible and read the whole book through from beginning to end. Then read it through again aloud, hearing the words and phrases, feeling them on your lips. If you are in a group, have different people read different sections so you hear and feel the full range of these beautiful, passionate words. As you read and listen, alone or in a group, pick out the phrases that most touch your soul. How do these phrases describe human relationships as well as human-divine relationship? How does the Song of Songs help you understand the connection between the sensual and the spiritual, between the erotic and the mystical?

3

PRAYING WHEN
OUR BODIES BETRAY US

When the body teaches us about the presence of God in our lives, we call the body "teacher." When we praise God in the body, we call it "prayer." When we find pleasure in the body's movements, sensuality, or sexuality, we call it "friend." When the body betrays us, we call it "enemy." Psalm 55 is a complaint about a friend's betrayal, and speaks to the anguish of the body's betrayal:

> It is not enemies who taunt me—
>   I could bear that;
> it is not adversaries who deal insolently with me—
>   I could hide from them.
> But it is you, my equal,
>   my companion, my familiar friend,
> with whom I kept pleasant company . . .
> (Ps. 55:12-14)

Our bodies may betray us in small ways. Our feet may stumble just as we enter a room and everyone has turned to greet us. Our hands may knock over a glass of wine at an elegant dinner party. We may lose our voices before an important lecture, or get the flu when on vacation. Sometimes we may feel that our bodies have betrayed us because they do not look as we would wish. Our hair is straight instead of curly. Our hips are wide instead of slim. We are too short or too tall, too thin or too fat, too freckled, too pale, too dark. We wish we were stronger, more coordinated, or more graceful. We long for our bodies to be different. We cannot accept them as they are.

In Frank Conroy's novel *Body and Soul*, the main character, Claude, discovers he is sterile. He walks aimlessly through the city of New York, trying to take in this new information.

That his body had betrayed him was a surprise, certainly, and yet there was something familiar in it, something that harked back to childhood and his anger at being thin and weak, his resentment at being trapped in his ridiculous skin. He had wanted nothing more than to transcend his body, to leave it behind through love and music. He had allowed himself to believe he was succeeding, but now, in an almost sinister fashion, hidden at a microscopic level, his old enemy had pulled him down. The gross, mute, stupid machine of his body was once again filling him with shame.[1]

Whether the betrayal by our bodies is through image or illness, accident or aging, and whether it is short-term or lifelong, our souls are affected as we experience alienation from our physical selves. When our bodies shame us, cause us pain, or do not work as they "should," we wish to distance ourselves. We may curse our bodies for the betrayal; we may punish them for the pain. We may separate body and soul hoping to transcend, rise above, ignore the body we experience as enemy. As the psalmist wrote about the desire to escape his enemy:

> And I say, "O that I had wings like a dove!
> I would fly away and be at rest . . . " (Ps. 55:6)

Aging and Dying

In our youth-centered culture, all signs of aging are often experienced as a betrayal by the body. We can no longer do as much in a day as we once could. If we sit in a low, soft chair, we have a hard time getting up. Our hands cannot open tight jars and we cannot lift our own luggage to the overhead bin in the airplane. We cannot read the phone book without our glasses, and we have a hard time hearing in a crowded restaurant. We lose hair, muscle tone, and energy. How might we pray into our older years?

"To live old is to not die young," is an old saying. With this in mind we might experience our aging as a reminder to pray our gratitude for the many years with which we have been gifted. Instead of complaining, we can thank God for the long life we have lived. We might pray for patience and compassion so as to treat our aging bodies with the same love with which we would respond to a cranky child. We might also pray for courage to face the unknowns, the losses, the mysteries of the aging and dying process. Our older years are a special time to renew and deepen our relationships with God. We have more time, but fewer responsibilities. We may become less attached to the material world.

In addition to praying for ourselves as we age, we may develop a practice of regular intercessory prayer. People who are no longer able to serve others as they did when they were younger may experience a deep loss and a feeling of uselessness and disconnection. They are unable to perform the many acts of loving kindness which formerly sustained them and gave their lives meaning.

An elderly woman in a retirement center spoke passionately of the work she had once done among the homeless. She had served meals, collected clothes, spoken to churches to raise money, and listened with an open heart to the stories of people living on the streets. She could no longer go to the shelter to be among the clients and staff, and she felt a profound sense of loss. The minister in charge of the program recognized her pain and asked for her help in another way. He wanted her to commit to daily prayers for the people of the streets, the staff at the center, and the churches who supported this unique ministry. Once again she was involved, valued, and connected, and was doing the important work of prayer. Her body could no longer serve, but her soul reached out in love.

Cardinal Bernardin, in the book *The Gift of Peace*, his personal reflections written shortly before he died of cancer, notes how important it is "to develop a strong prayer life in our best moments so that we can be sustained in our weaker moments."[2] He then shares his own experience of being unable to pray in the midst of serious illness and extreme pain:

> I wanted to pray, but the physical discomfort was overwhelming. I remember saying to the friends who visited me, "Pray while you're well, because if you wait until you're sick, you might not be able to do it." They looked at me, astonished. I said, "I'm in so much discomfort that I can't focus on prayer. My faith is still present. There is nothing wrong with my faith, but in terms of prayer, I'm just too preoccupied with the pain. I'm going to remember that I must pray when I am well!"[3]

As Cardinal Bernardin moved toward his death, he held on to the passage from Matthew's Gospel: "Come to me, all you that are weary and are carrying heavy burdens, and I will give you rest" (Matt. 11:28). As he reflected on this passage he found comfort in the rest promised and the burden shared. He mused that "perhaps the ultimate burden is death itself."[4] When he reflected further on the text, he noticed that Jesus did not promise to take away our burdens, but rather promised to help us carry them. He then makes this profound statement about death: "If we let go of ourselves — and our own resources — and allow the Lord to help us, we will be able to see death not as an enemy or as a threat but as a friend."[5]

Praying for Our Bodies

Cardinal Bernardin's experience teaches us by example the possibility of seeing death as a friend rather than an enemy. Henri Nouwen teaches us a similar lesson about our bodies when he writes: "You have come to see your body as an enemy to be conquered. But God wants you to befriend your body. . . . "⁶ One way to befriend our bodies is to pray for them, asking God's blessing upon our bodies and expressing gratitude for our embodiment. But praying for our bodies becomes difficult when our bodies betray us and we experience our bodies as enemies.

Jesus told us, "Love your enemies and pray for those who persecute you" (Matt. 5:44). Are we able to obey this commandment when our body is our enemy? Can we pray when we feel that our soul is being imprisoned by the enemy? In times of the most difficult betrayal some people do find ways to pray with and for their bodies. We can learn from their stories of prayer.

Trish

"I'm convinced that I will walk again." Trish, a Roman Catholic, spoke those words from her wheelchair four months after major back surgery that left her not paralyzed but with no coordination or strength in her legs. She would need to learn to walk all over again as an adult. "I know that my faith and the faith of others who have prayed for me have helped to get me where I am. I could so easily have ended up paralyzed."

Trish is no stranger to a body that has not always cooperated. At age nine she was diagnosed with scoliosis and a fluid-filled cyst in her spine. In addition she had a mild case of polio. "When I was in elementary school, I could not skip and run and play. After surgeries, I still couldn't because my back was fragile. I learned to be an observer and I think that is one way of being with God. Observing for me became a prayer of awareness and gratitude."

As a teenager, Trish walked with a slight limp. But her physical condition did not keep her from active parenting. She was able to lift and carry both of her children in her twenties and thirties. As she grew older, her body lost some of its strength and her scoliosis gradually became active again. In the past year, she had lost her sense of balance and had fallen frequently. She suffered from pain and fatigue. She knew something had to be done. That something was spinal cord surgery.

One of the ways Trish prepared for surgery was to ask people to pray for her. She requested prayers from friends and family and from the religious community of which she is a member. Four hundred people in that community shared her request with members of other communities and parishes. "There were many, many people praying for me that didn't know me and whom I didn't know at all," she recalls. Trish believes she received support and protection through those many prayers. "I think that what those prayers did for me was to shield me from terrible fear and anxiety. I also attribute my relative freedom from pain to those numerous prayers."

For her own prayers, Trish turned to the rosary. Although the rosary had not been a constant in her prayer life, she had found it a comfort in times of stress. "As a child, I had a lot of illness and I used to say the rosary a lot. When I get in a really difficult situation, I always go back to those familiar beads and words." Trish found praying to Mary, the mother figure, very comforting. She would begin praying the rosary at night and often fall asleep before she had finished. "There's something very comforting about falling asleep in the presence of God, of the Virgin. I didn't go to sleep in fear. I didn't go to sleep in anxiety. I may have started the prayer that way, but as I continued praying the feelings left me. The rosary does that for me."

Now Trish is home, and in the long process of healing and learning to walk again. Her exercises and physical therapy and, more recently, standing and then walking with a walker take up much of her time and energy. "Sometimes my body makes me angry. I get so frustrated with it that I just want to scream." Trish doesn't give in to her anger because she feels it would use up the energy she needs for her exercise routine, which already requires much self-discipline. Instead, she turns to God for strength and courage. "I actively ask God a lot for help, particularly when I feel wobbly and shaky in the sense of learning to walk again. It's really scary, so when I get up on the walker and I am going from here to there, I almost without fail ask for God's help." Trish depends on God's presence simply to keep on keeping on—one step at a time.

"There is an old saying that 'we all die alone,' even though we may have people around us. I have discovered that we recover alone, too. People can give me lots of encouragement, and the surgeons can be reassuring, but the reality is, it's me and my body and God. No one is here with me all day long doing exercises. If I choose to lie on my back all day and do nothing, or watch TV all day, or eat all day or stare out the window all day, it's not going to hurt or help anyone except me. I am alone with God. It's me saying to God, "One more step. Help me do one more step. Make that step secure."

Trish struggles with her body becoming the center of her life. She knows that her recovery has to be the focus of her world, but not to the exclusion of other interests, other people, other concerns. She wishes to remain God-centered rather than body-centered. In this regard, she has become aware of a strange paradox: As she focuses on her body and her recovery, her soul is being freed.

In her solitude and in the routine of exercising, Trish has had many hours for self-reflection. She became aware of the many professional roles and activities she had been involved in that no longer fed her soul. She recognized that her reputation and the high regard in which other people held her had given her an identity in which she had become trapped. Although grateful for all these gifts, Trish has resigned from most of her responsibilities and is waiting to see where she will be led.

"I think what's happened to me during these four months is a freeing process in which the spirit kind of takes over. I'm finding out about liberating my true self. I continue to feel that there's more to me than I've discovered and used before. I don't know yet what that is or how I will continue to liberate it, but it is what I want, and I'm getting increasingly comfortable with the process."

Brian

"Load of hay, load of hay, make a wish and turn away." This saying from childhood was Brian's first prayer response when he was diagnosed with HIV in 1988. "My wish was that they would find a cure, so that people, myself included, would not have to die."

Brian considers himself a man of little faith. He is not sure there is a God "out there." He wonders whether prayer "works." He is surrounded by people—family and friends—who have deep faith. "It's always been something I've admired and envied in a lot of ways, because I take a much more intellectual approach to the whole thing." His intellectual approach has led him to discussions and readings and musings about the nature of God, the person of Jesus, the meaning of life and death. He is not willing to call this searching "faith," because, as he says, "If I had faith, then I feel like I wouldn't have so many unanswered questions."

Brian at first did not tell his family about his diagnosis. Only his partner, Dale, and a few close friends knew. He also decided to tell the minister of his family's church, because he knew his mother would need support when she found out. He had attended that church on occasion. "I would take my grandmother, then I would separate from the people and the worship. My purpose was not going to church for myself—I went for Grandma."

"When I told the minister what the situation was, he didn't say, 'Oh, you need to pray to God about it.' He didn't hit me with any religious stuff at all. He just gave me compassion. He gave me unconditional love, which we talk about all the time but very rarely get. He met me with real, true, unconditional love."

After Brian's grandmother died, he continued to attend church. Dale, who had come from a religious background, joined him. Shortly thereafter, they both formally joined the church. "At Sunday worship, we have silent prayer time and that's the only time that I really can say I pray. I begin with, 'God, if you are out there and if you are listening . . . ' Then I would tell God that I was furious about my diagnosis and my illness and demand to know why God had let this happen and rattle off all my anger and complaints. Then my mind would take over and say, 'This really is not God's fault,' and then I would think, 'Okay, Brian, this is what you need to do in your life—

you need to make plans, you need to relax, you need to have fun. You need
to live like they always say: You should live every day as your last. Well,
buddy, every day may be your last—now it's time.'

"This became a regular Sunday battle. I would be furious at the beginning of prayer, and very quickly I would move to making plans, and then the
anger kind of went away. It took a long time for me not to have that first rant-
ing part at the beginning of the prayers, but over time I actually didn't do that
part any more. Then the prayer was, 'Okay, God, if you are out there, then
give me the courage to deal with this.'" Brian also found himself praying for
hope, for strength, for patience, and, when the time comes, to die gracefully.

As Brian struggled with his prayer life and with his relationship to "the
God who might not be there," he began to examine his life and his priorities.
Joy became his priority—things that gave himself and others joy. He turned
his attention to creating a joyful, committed relationship with Dale. He told
his family about his illness and then planned a trip. "I took money out of my
savings plan, and I took my brother and his wife and their kids and Dale to
Hawaii. We went for three weeks. I used up all the Frequent Flyer miles. We
went to three islands, and we went to enjoy the moment. Before the diagnosis, I never would have done that!" Brian was deeply moved by the amount
of support given to him by his entire family. "It was much, much more than
I had anticipated. I now encourage others to break silence and tell their families of their diagnoses earlier than I did."

Brian became more active in the life of the church, connecting to members of the congregation, giving and receiving support. The Sunday church
service included a time for sharing of joys and concerns, and Brian learned
about praying for others and began to accept that others were praying for
him. He and his mother and Dale joined a small group in the church that met
monthly to discuss a book they were reading together and to talk openly
about their lives. They shared food and ideas and laughter and tears. In this
group, Brian experienced the joy of community.

Brian is now on new medicine that has lowered the level of virus in his
system to traces. He has gone off disability and returned to full-time work.
He and Dale are readjusting to the possibility of a long life together. "We are
now together for the long haul. Our prayers are still about hope, still about
joy, and still about relationship, but the context of our prayers has changed,
because we are facing a future."

Regaining his health has not turned Brian into a "believer." He still
wonders about the efficacy of prayer. He struggles with theological questions and images of God. He doubts his own faith. But Brian recognizes
how his life has changed in the past ten years. He has discovered the importance of relationships and community. He has learned to pray alone and

with others. He has poured energy into the people and activities of his local church. He has become a man committed to joy: "For me, having HIV has not been a bad thing. It's actually been a positive, because it has made me look differently at my life."

Nancy

Nancy was thirty-three years old and nineteen weeks pregnant with her first child, a girl they had named Catherine, when she knew something was terribly wrong. She and her husband, Dan, went to the doctor's office for an ultrasound test. As the picture came on the screen they could not tell what they were looking at, or whether the image was normal or not. The nurses would not tell them what they saw, but would only call other people in. Finally the doctor arrived and, after a long look at the screen, told them that their baby had died. The infant's body cavity had never closed and her tiny organs were floating in Nancy's womb. The doctors were unable then or later to explain what had happened, although they believed that whatever had gone wrong had happened at six or seven weeks. They said it was amazing that Catherine had lived as long as she had.

"When things began to go wrong, I prayed that I wouldn't lose her," Nancy said. "But when everything happened, I stopped praying. My most desperate hour was having my milk come in after I had lost Catherine. I remember getting up and my nightgown was drenched. I was wandering around my house looking and crying: 'Where's my baby, where's my baby?' If I lost her, she's got to be somewhere. I slid into depression. I felt like I wanted to die. I didn't want to kill myself, but I felt, 'I need to be with her. If she's out there, if she's in heaven, if she's with God—I need to be there with her.'"

Nancy was angry at her body. It felt like an enemy that had betrayed her. For years she had longed to become pregnant. "I thought there was this sort of secret club of motherhood that I really wanted to be a part of. I couldn't wait for my pregnancy to show. I wanted to be big. I wanted to get into maternity clothes. When that was ripped away, I felt that my body had failed. I kept thinking, 'What's wrong with me? What's wrong with me?'"

People prayed for Nancy in her grief. Some of the prayers were comforting, and some were not. When people told her the miscarriage was God's will, she responded internally with rage. "I thought, 'God would never want this for anyone.'" Others told her it was God's way of saving her from having a deformed child. Another told her to be comforted by the fact that God really knew about this because God had lost his son. "I know people felt awkward and didn't know what to say. I know they were not trying to hurt me. I know I was really angry and frustrated and grieving, so anything anybody said didn't sit well."

In the midst of Nancy's despair, the prayers of presence were the ones that helped her. One friend canceled all her appointments when she heard of the tragedy and simply arrived at Nancy's front door, threw her arms around her, and said, "I'm sorry." Another friend called her and said, "Nancy, I just wanted to tell you that if you ever want to talk about this experience, I had a similar thing happen to me years ago. I'm available to talk and listen." Nancy's mother was with her when her milk came in. Instead of telling her to allow the doctors to give her a shot to dry her breasts, her mother encouraged her to feel the experience. "Look at it this way, Nancy. Your breasts are practicing, and they are really working, so the next time you will know exactly what to do."

With the comfort of family and friends and time, Nancy began to look toward the future. She befriended her body, and she did everything she could to become strong and healthy. She began to pray again. "I was raised Episcopalian and love all the rituals that are associated with that. But I think my religious views are very broad and encompassing. I feel deep spiritual connections on many levels. Playing music, painting, being outdoors, being with my children—all are forms of prayer for me."

Nancy and Dan now have three sons, and ten years have passed since Catherine's death. But she has not been forgotten. Dan had planted an evergreen tree in their yard as a way of marking their loss. "Every year, Dan decorates it with Christmas lights. That's Catherine's tree—and we all go out and just be around it, and the boys know that's their sister's tree."

With the tenth anniversary of her loss, a poem began to take shape in Nancy's mind and heart. As it formed, a melody came with it. Soon the poem/song took on a life of its own. "I would start out singing this every morning in the bathtub. It was my prayer. It was my way to start the day, and I did this day after day after day."

With the help of her colleagues, Nancy recorded her prayer and then shared the piece in a performance called "Women's Work," designed to explore the use of different mediums to express the deeper processes of creativity. "I used my piece (called "Catherine") as an expression and resolution of feeling the very delicate line between life and death that birth seems to always bring to us."

Catherine

I still have a question:
Who found her?
If I lost her, who found her?
Is she still floating out there, unembodied,
In cold, dark space
Hovering round?

If I lost her, who found her?

I longed for your face the most,
To close my eyes and feel moist heat,
Kitten's breath bathe my skin,
And I would lick you clean,
Turning you with my nose.

If I lost you, who found you?

When I lost you, I was adrift with tears,
An anchor rope torn from my belly,
Breasts, flooding with steaming milk,
Searching for your mouth,
Hungry for you
As you were for me.

If I lost you, who found you?

I felt you move that night,
Weeping as the music washed over me,
Brittle notes of the Holocaust
Leaking from the lowest octaves of the piano,
Darkest, most private tones
Penetrating my womb,
Moving our daughter in salty water,
Rocking in warm, dark space,
Rippling with doubts about life beyond this warm well.

If I lost you, who found you?

Years later in a dream
You called me up on a telephone
To ask me how I was;
And I replied,
Just fine; how are you?
And you answered,
I am at the fourth level and
I am filled
With wonder.

Alleluia, Alleluia
Alleluia, Alleluia

Roy

"Nineteen years ago, on October 15, I was diagnosed as having multiple sclerosis. My first reaction to the diagnosis was to slip into a quiet, passive state of mind—what Thoreau once called 'a life of quiet desperation.' I don't remember being angry with God, but somehow I resigned myself to a life with no purpose or meaning. This went on for several years."

During these years of "quiet desperation," Roy lost significant use of his legs, he struggled with great pain, his marriage ended, and he moved to an assisted-living unit in a nursing home. Roy is a retired Presbyterian minister who found solace not in Christian prayer but rather in Buddhist teachings and meditation.

"My oldest son introduced me to an author who helped set my course of healing, not curing, because there is a vast difference between being cured and being healed. The book was *Healing into Life and Death* by Stephen Levine. Levine taught me not to hate disease, not to be resigned to it, not simply to adjust to it, but actually to love it. He said never, never raise the 'why' questions, because they are simply not answerable, but to deal with the 'what' questions. Learn to know your disease, learn to know your own body, and ultimately learn to love the pain."

Levine also introduced Roy to three Buddhist teachings that have guided his healing process over the years. The first was to love himself. No one needed his love more than he did. The second teaching was to understand that the more difficult the challenge, the greater the reward will be in meeting and conquering it. And the third teaching was that he was the path of his own healing—not the doctor, not his family, not Jesus. With these teachings in mind and heart, Roy prepared a system by which he could respond to his illness.

"I decided there was no better course of action known to me than to invest heavily in others—their welfare and their fulfillment. My daughter had once given me a banner that reads, 'Grow where you are planted.' Surely I had been planted in a place I had never dreamed I would be spending any time at all. So I volunteered to help in any way the nursing home staff thought I could assist. I prepared a program called 'World Issues,' in which we discussed news from all over the globe. I was asked to serve on the food committee, and, since I had a three-wheeled, battery-powered chair with a basket, I could hardly avoid being asked to deliver the mail!"

Roy became involved with residents and staff, engaging them in informal conversations and counseling. Ultimately he was given the Volunteer of the Year award, the first time it had ever been given to a resident. Roy said of the award that it was "a very meaningful and beautiful gesture on their part. However, we all know that in giving we receive. Every hour spent in every activity rewarded me with countless blessings and enriched relationships. Quite unconsciously I was receiving all the tools I needed to cope. No, I was receiving the tools I needed to live a rich life."

Roy is now married to Martha, whom he met at an Elderhostel. "One of the matters that drew us together was learning each other's commitment to volunteering." Roy attended a ten-week course at the Iliff School of Theology dealing with theological developments of the nineteenth and twentieth centuries. "Here I sat, among fifty young people the age of my oldest grandson, lapping up all the information I could gather. A most rewarding adventure!" Roy's most recent accomplishment was learning to ski. The state MS society arranged for interested members to become involved in a handicap skiing program at Winter Park Ski Resort. "During the last thirty minutes of my second session, I learned how to ski! This seventy-seven-year-old curmudgeon learned to ski on a bi-ski, which has a seat fastened to it. It was fantastic!"

Roy does not pray in any traditional Christian way. He continues to meditate regularly, his favorite forms being a "Loving Kindness" meditation and a "Forgiveness" meditation. Roy and Martha offer a thanksgiving prayer every morning. He has grave doubts about intercessory prayer and does not pray for himself or others, although he knows that others pray for him. For Roy, his life of service is his prayer. He says, "I am of the opinion that my life belongs to the whole community and as long as I live it is my privilege to do for it whatever I can. I want to be thoroughly used up when I die, because the harder I work, the more I live."

Karen

Karen separated her body and soul at age twelve, when she was sexually abused and raped by one of her teachers. Her body became her enemy, and she treated it with scorn. In her teen years, she gained weight, and she ignored the symptoms of early arthritis and fibromyalgia, a painful muscle disease. "My muscles have never worked right. I thought it was just because I was fat. I forced myself to do difficult physical things that I considered normal, just to prove I wasn't lazy. I might be fat, but I wasn't lazy!"

Karen's enmity with her body continued into her adult years. "I wouldn't take care of my body and treat it nicely because it was so bad, it was ugly, it wasn't nice to me, and it hurt all the time. I tried to 'rise above it' (one of the dumbest phrases ever invented), and in so doing caused further damage." By the age of 35, Karen was severely overweight, exhausted, and in constant pain. She had only three hours of energy and productivity a day.

Eventually, Karen stopped trying to 'rise above' her physicality, and began to face what was going on in her body and soul. She became more aggressive with her doctors, and finally her fibromyalgia was correctly diagnosed. She entered therapy to deal with her memories of sexual abuse. She credits her faith in God, her connection to Jesus, and her active prayer life with helping her to find the courage to begin the healing process—and the strength to continue it, because healing has been a long and rugged road.

Karen cannot imagine going back into her memories without the presence of God and the companionship of Jesus. "I took Jesus by the hand every time I went into a memory." Although many sexual abuse survivors report feeling abandoned by God during abuse, Karen recognized God's presence even in the midst of the violence. "I could feel that I was not alone. Something was helping me, physically and emotionally holding me—not removing me from the situation, but comforting me. That is how God is present with us and why I believe God doesn't stop abusers who won't let God in. The man who abused me chose to do that and chose to allow the evil side of him to take over and not let God in. God can't go where God's not invited."

As Karen continued to be healed from her sexual abuse, she realized how her physical problems had been exacerbated by her disassociation from her body. She knew she would have to make friends with her body. She began to pray for her body. "When you pray for an enemy, it's hard to keep the enemy at a distance. When I started praying for my body, I had to confront it and be there with it. That's what's so amazing about prayer: What you pray for becomes a part of who you are! So my body had to become a part of who I am."

As Karen reconnects her body and soul, she is discovering how care for her physical and emotional well-being are dependent on each other. "When I entered a memory, my body would go back to that time and feel the pain. When I remembered the rape, my body would feel the whole thing inside and out. Then the pain of the emotion and the pain of betrayal would hit me all at once. I discovered that when I worked through the emotional pain, my body would heal. I realized that we, my body and I, were on the same team."

Therapeutic massage has helped Karen continue the healing of body and soul. Karen and Marie, her massage therapist, approach their sessions prayerfully. Karen spends time in meditation before the sessions, turning control of the healing over to God. They do not talk during the sessions, but Marie's hands find places that are in need of healing, and Karen feels the heat of release. "I would give up the pain of my memories on her table. She would literally massage it right out of my arm, right out of my shoulders— gone, and it hasn't come back. Massage has become body prayer for me."

Today Karen says that she and her body are friends. "I pray for my body, and my body prays for me. " Through exercise she is working out the muscle pain and the weariness and the chronic fatigue that is associated with fibromyalgia. She listens to her body and heeds what it tells her by giving

herself intermittent periods of relaxation and meditation, or going home a little early to have time in the spa, or taking an extra hour of sleep when it is
needed.

She is still working on her weight. "I need to listen to what my body
really wants to eat and then fix it what it wants and needs. This will come in
time. I have learned to be patient with my body and let it heal at its own
rate." Karen does not pray in terms of "cure." She prays in gratitude for
God's continuous presence from the beginning of her life, during the abuse,
and through the many years of pain, struggle, and denial. She knows that
God has accompanied her on every step of her healing journey. Karen prays
for a deeper and deeper relationship with God from which she trusts will
come complete healing, body and soul.

Healing and Wholeness

"There is a vast difference between being cured and being healed," exclaimed
Roy, at the beginning of his story. Karen echoes that understanding at the
end of her story. All of the stories you have just read are about healing, not
about curing. None of the people has been cured of his or her illnesses. Trish
may walk again, but she will still have scoliosis. Nancy may have carried
three children to term, but Catherine died before she lived. Brian may now
be well, thanks to the new medication, but his positive HIV diagnosis still
stands. We will not be cured of our aging, and Cardinal Bernardin died of
his cancer.

Sometimes when the body betrays, there are medical cures. Surgery
repairs the faulty heart valve, antibiotics take care of the sinus infection, broken bones usually mend completely with time and medical intervention.
Medicine can also balance and stabilize people, for example, insulin for the
diabetic, thyroid medication for over- or underactive thyroids, hormone
replacement therapy for women in menopause.

Sometimes when the body betrays, there are miraculous cures.
Occasionally we hear of a situation when all the doctors have given up any
hope of recovery and yet a person's inevitable movement toward death is
reversed. A person with cancer not only goes into remission, but all traces of
cancer disappear. Another person emerges from a long coma with clarity of
mind and full use of the body, when such a recovery was not deemed possible.

When anyone is cured, medically or miraculously, we rejoice and praise
God. But the absence of a cure is not an indication that healing is not taking
place. A woman reported that when her mother was diagnosed with cancer,
she and all her family began to pray. "My mother was not cured, the cancer
did not go away, and she died within two years of the diagnosis. But my

mother and I were estranged before her illness. Her need of me brought me home. My mother was not cured, but our relationship was healed."

Healing is about right relationship and reconciliation. Mother and daughter overcome their differences. Trish connects to her deepest self. Roy learns to love his pain. Nancy loves her body and becomes its friend. Brian reaches out to family and community with joy. Karen prays for her body and discovers that her body and soul are "on the same team." Seniors experience their aging bodies as the blessing of a long life. Cardinal Bernardin discovered with the Lord's help that death could become a friend.

Healing brings an experience of wholeness. Wholeness, like healing, is an experience of right relationship with God, oneself, and one's neighbor. Wholeness is not about perfection. None of us—young or old, ill or healthy, disabled or temporarily abled—has a perfect body. Our culture would have us believe that perfecting our bodies is our goal and that such perfection is the way to happiness. Some traditional Christian teaching maintains that by denying and/or transcending our imperfect bodies we will perfect our souls and achieve spiritual happiness. But perfection is not the issue and not the goal. In fact, the pursuit of perfection can stand in the way of the process of healing and wholeness.

Nancy Eiesland gives a powerful image of the imperfect body in her book, *The Disabled God*. Dr. Eiesland writes out of her own experience of lifelong disability and attacks the oppressive myth of the perfect body. She says that the resurrected Jesus reveals himself to be the disabled God when he appears to his disciples and followers to display his wounded and impaired hands and feet (Luke 24:36-39). "The disabled God is not only the One from heaven but the revelation of true personhood, underscoring the reality that full personhood is fully compatible with the experience of disability."[7]

Dr. Eiesland's theology and imagery presents us with a vision of the imperfect body of the resurrected Jesus. Her image guides us to accepting imperfection as an integral part of the human experience and as fully acceptable to God. When we are able to move to this depth of acceptance, we no longer seek to perfect the imperfect body. Instead we seek to embrace the wholeness of the one within the body and celebrate the healing power of love.

Rachel Naomi Remen wrote the following poem about her experience of the process of healing and wholeness:

O
body!
For 41 years
1,573 experts with
14,355 combined years of training
have failed
to
cure
your wounds.
Deep inside
I
am
whole.[8]

ACTIVITIES FOR REFLECTION AND DISCUSSION

1. We are all growing old. Even as we sit here we are aging. To connect to this process experientially, spend some time finding pictures of yourself in different ages and stages. Study these pictures and remember when and how you treated your body as a friend and when you experienced your body as an enemy. Then reflect on your present physical condition and ask yourself how you might befriend your body now. What does your body need from you? Are you willing to give your body what it needs? Is there a prayer that forms in your mind or your heart, or through your hands or your actions that would invite God into the sacred task of befriending your body?

2. Think of someone in your life who is physically challenged, either temporarily or permanently. Ask if you might interview him or her about the role of prayer in relationship to the body. Approach the interview prayerfully with an open mind and an open heart. Go to listen and learn, not to teach. Some questions you might consider are:

- How do you talk to God about your particular physical issue?
- Do you pray for your body? If so, what is your prayer?
- Are you ever angry with God about what has happened?
- Are there books, or devotional materials, or particular Bible passages that have helped you?
- What has your body and this particular physical experience taught you about your relationship to God?

3. Matthew 5:48 is commonly translated: "Be perfect, therefore, as your heavenly Father is perfect." Find this passage in a number of different Bible translations. Look also at the parallel verse in the Gospel of Luke, chapter 6, verse 36. What do these verses and the lessons surrounding them teach you

about wholeness? As your understanding of wholeness expands, begin looking for images of wholeness in your daily life. Notice how images of wholeness are different from images of perfection.

4

HUMOR, LAUGHTER,
AND PLAYFUL PRAYER

Balloons were everywhere! On the dining room tables, peeking from behind doors. Seven balloons were in one retreatant's bed, two at the entrance to the chapel. A gift balloon was taped to each priest's door. A huge bouquet of balloons danced over the altar when Father Bob said Mass. And a balloon was tied to everyone's car as we left the retreat house on our closing day. The balloons seemed to have a life of their own, appearing and disappearing and bringing smiles of delight to everyone.

I had no idea what would happen when I introduced balloons to eighteen retreatants on the second day of a five-day silent retreat titled "The Practice of Presence." I saw the balloons as a teaching tool, a way to experiment with being attentive and inattentive, present and absent to something in our lives. The retreatants played with their balloons, keeping them in motion first alone and then with a partner. They discovered in their bodies what happened when they attended to the balloon, and what happened if their attention wandered. They discovered that working hard at being present often caused resentment and tension. They learned that an easy presence, a light touch, was the essence of holy attention.

Pleased with the learning experience, I told the retreatants to keep their balloons to practice with, and offered more if anyone's broke. I had no idea that the balloons would become a retreat theme following us everywhere. I had a few moments of worry, because we were but a small group in a fairly large retreat house. There were a number of people on private retreats, community people coming in for Mass, staff working at the business of running a spirituality center. Would our play offend them? Would our surprise and delight interfere with their prayer? Were we having too much fun? We were told later that the light spirit of play that accompanied the moving balloons had not been experienced for a long time. There was gratitude that play and laughter had returned to the retreat house.

Christians have the reputation of being serious people not prone to good humor, laughter, or play. One early church father preached adamantly against fun:

> This world is not a theatre in which we can laugh, and we are not assembled together in order to burst into peals of laughter, but to weep for our sins. . . . It is not God who gives us the chance to play, but the devil.[1]

In our own country, the Puritans did much to continue this reputation of dourness, with long hours spent in church, rigorous daily prayers, and restrictions against music and dancing and bright colors. Holiness seemed to be equated with judgment, suffering, and severity. However, this serious attitude taken to the extreme was recognized by John Wesley as a danger and a sin in itself when he said: "Sour Godliness is the devil's religion." And Martin Luther was reported to have said, "If you're not allowed to laugh in heaven, then I don't want to go there."[2]

Many people I know who are very intentional in their religious and spiritual practices welcome lightness and humor, laughter and play. When I was a young woman, I spent some time with a large Mormon family. One evening I joined them for dinner at a lovely restaurant. The talk was lively, with much laughter. The waiter asked if we wanted drinks, and the mother of the family smiled at him, saying, "We don't drink." When he inquired if we needed an ashtray, the father said quietly, "We don't smoke." After an excellent meal, we were offered coffee, and everyone said together with great humor, "We don't drink coffee." The waiter then hesitantly asked, "Would you like dessert?" The teenaged son piped up with great glee, "Now *that* is something we *do*!"

Recently I observed a family of four waiting at Denver International Airport. They were clearly members of a religious group. The man and the boy were dressed in dark, formal clothes. The mother and daughter wore long, plain dresses and black bonnets. And they were eating ice cream with so much delight I could not help but smile to watch them. They exclaimed and laughed and traded bites, all the time looking around with great excitement at their new surroundings. These were certainly not dour religious folk!

Yet even when we are eager and ready to include joy and good humor and play in our individual and family lives, we are often hesitant to bring the same qualities of fun into our relationship with God. Is it because we are afraid that God has no sense of humor? If we want to bring play and laughter into our relationship with God, we may need to expand our image of God to include the quality of fun.

Mark Liebenow, author of *Is There Fun after Paul?* creates an image of God from biblical stories that helps in our search for a playful image of God:

If God didn't love to laugh, then why create giraffes and rhinoceroses? Why tease with the wisdom of this world by choosing to work through the simple, the foolish, the powerless as God has done so often? Why choose Moses to be the speaker for the Israelites when Moses stumbled over his tongue? Why make the Israelites the "Chosen People" when they lived in the geographical doormat of the Middle East? And why choose a wishy-washy person like Peter, give him a name that means "Rock," and say, "Upon this wishy-washy person I will build my church?" Who is God kidding? Who is going to believe and trust in a God like this? Who indeed, except that God must have a profoundly deep sense of humor. It just doesn't make sense otherwise.[3]

I understand "sense of humor" to mean a light perspective on life, an ability to see the comic in creation and humanity, and a willingness to laugh at ourselves. Human relationships cannot survive without a sense of humor. Even when our relationships are difficult and uncomfortable and we have to "work" on them to ease the struggles, clear the communication, allow ourselves to know and be known, we can laugh and discover the humor in our predicaments. So it is with our relationship with God. If all our prayers are solemn, all our conversations with God serious, all of our listening for God attuned to the "important," we have missed the opportunity of light, silly, playful prayer. When we bring our humor to a God with a sense of humor, who knows what might happen next!

> O humorous, playful, fun-loving God—
> Knock me over with your ridiculous creations.
> Roll with me in laughter at the ways of the world.
> Push me over the edge of my seriousness
>   into your laughing, loving arms. Amen

Playing with God

I imagine that our relationship with God is somewhat like children playing hide and seek. At times, we try to hide from God, looking for the perfect place in which we can be alone and out of reach. At other times we jump from our hiding place crying to God, "Find me! Find me!" as little children do when waiting to be found becomes intolerable. When God seems to be hidden from us, we go seeking for God, crying, "Do not hide your face from me!" Sometimes God seems so cleverly hidden from us that we despair. But if we keep on seeking, we find that God has been waiting patiently, and greets us with delight, knowing that ultimately we will come.

Play is about spontaneity, imagination, and fun. Watch young children at play. They run and they chase; they fall down and get up. They cry and they laugh. They argue and they encourage. They pretend they are horses or doctors or race-car drivers. They move from one fantasy to another, with each new imagery experience spiraling out of their previous activity. They are in the moment, they are going nowhere, they are fully engaged.

In contrast to children, adults often work at play. We schedule time to play. We play because it is good for the family or a way to relax. We search for things that are "fun" to do. We play to win. However, adults *can* return to the freedom of childhood and discover spontaneous play in the midst of our daily lives. Adults can be open to the possibility that being with God might be playful and fun. A light and playful attitude can lead us to new forms of prayer.

A pastoral counselor found a new way to pray when he rode his bicycle home along a familiar route after a long day of seeing clients. As he pedaled he remembered all the people he had seen that day and all of their concerns and problems. He began to imagine "placing" these people in various houses as he rode along. He would match the person to the house and gently place them inside. When he arrived home, all the people and their concerns had been lovingly put aside. He realized that this fantasy was a form of prayer. "As I placed each person in a different house, I was actually turning them and their concerns over to God," he remembers. For this man, living in the moment created a playful form of intercessory prayer.

We must be alert for the old voices that try to keep us only serious and solemn about prayer. These old teachings almost pulled one woman away from a very powerful prayer form. She gradually created a morning routine where she went from her bed to the most comfortable chair in her apartment, which looked out over the mountains. She wrapped herself in her grandmother's quilt and sipped hot tea. Sometimes she remained in silence; sometimes she played music. She might write in her journal, or she might not. She told me that she was having trouble calling her morning time "prayer." "I do feel connected to God, and the experience of God-with-me continues through my day," she said. "But I'm not sure I am really praying, because it is so easy to do and is so much fun." With time she overcame her hesitancy and continued her practice. Later she was able to respond when asked about her morning prayer: "I simply delight in God."

One way to practice playing with God is simply to invite God into our playful moments. When we play with our children, or our pets, remember that God plays with us. When we have fun with our friends, imagine God as part of the activities and the playful conversation. When we get silly alone or with a loved one, try to imagine being silly with God. Play, fun, and silliness are all part of our human relationships. We can discover simple ways to make them part of our relationship with God.

As we become more comfortable playing with God, we may find fun and humor creeping into our verbal prayers. We may begin to tell God funny stories, incidents that made us laugh. We might talk to God in a joking way, or call God to account with humor as St. Teresa of Àvila was said to have done. One story tells of Teresa traveling around Spain on a cold and rainy night. When her wagon broke down, she and her companions were far from help. As she looked at the damage, she looked upward and raised her fist to God. She was heard to shout: "If this is the way you treat your friends, no wonder you have so few!"

When I was little and a fly would be swooping and buzzing around the kitchen, my grandmother would go after it with a dish towel quoting the humorous poet Ogden Nash: "God in His wisdom made the fly and then forgot to tell us why." Her actions and her words always made me laugh, and remembering the image today still brings me a smile of delight. I now believe that those times of buzzing flies, flashing dish towels, and laughter were times of prayer. In my grandmother's own unique way, she had invited God into our kitchen.

Laughter

There is an old saying that tears and laughter come from the same place in the soul. Maybe this is why they are so often linked in the Bible. Ecclesiastes tells us there is a time to weep and a time to laugh (3:4). Luke offers the promise of laughter when he writes "Blessed are you who weep now, for you will laugh" (6:21). The psalmist sings of the laughter and joy that came when the Lord restored the fortunes of Zion: "Then our mouth was filled with laughter, and our tongue with shouts of joy" (126:2).

Laughter and weeping are also linked in the opposite direction. Proverbs tell us that "even in laughter the heart is sad, and the end of joy is grief" (14:13). James writes: "Lament, and mourn and weep. Let your laughter be turned to mourning and your joy into dejection" (4:9). And Luke reverses himself, saying: "Woe to you who are laughing now, for you will mourn and weep" (6:25b).

A complicated story of laughter occurs in Genesis 18 and 21. Sarah had mourned her entire life, because she was unable to bear a child. Then, when she was in her advanced years, the Lord promised her a son. Sarah laughed to herself, saying, "After I have grown old, and my husband is old, shall I have pleasure?" The Lord asked why Sarah laughed. "Is anything too wonderful for the Lord?" Then Sarah denied her laughter because she was afraid. When Sarah did conceive and give birth, Abraham named their son

Isaac, which means laughter. And Sarah proclaimed: "God has brought laughter for me; everyone who hears will laugh with me."

Who among us has not laughed and then denied it? Maybe as a child you laughed at something an adult did not find funny. "Did you laugh?" you were asked. "No, ma'am. I burped!" Maybe we got the giggles in church. People turned to stare disapprovingly. We would pull a straight face and pretend someone else laughed. And so Sarah, hearing of a baby in her old age, laughed with disbelief. Notice that God did not punish Sarah for her laughter. Rather, God reminded her that *anything* is possible for the Lord.

Sarah's words after the birth of Isaac are significant not only to her story but to our understanding of the gift of laughter. Even with all the confusion of laughing and not laughing, the story of Isaac's birth proclaims laughter as created by God, and laughter as a call to community. Sarah said, "God has brought laughter for me." She knew Isaac was a gift from God. Sarah said: "Everyone who hears will laugh with me." She knew that her family and friends would delight in the baby. They too would be amazed. They would not laugh "at" her. The community would come together and laugh "with" her in her joy.

Sarah's community was filled with laughter and joy and love. Rick Bernardo, in his article "A Serious Meditation on Laughter," wrote that "it's difficult not to love someone when you are laughing with them."[4] Have you experienced the love that comes with shared laughter? Maybe an intimate moment with a loved one when the same thing strikes you both funny at the same time and you shout with laughter. Maybe a family dinner when a funny story is told and young and old alike break into laughter. Sometimes laughter is shared with others in even larger groups.

When I was teaching elementary school, there would be days when laughter would begin somewhere in the room. Maybe two children together found something funny. Soon others were asking, "What's so funny?" and the original laughers would try to speak but were overcome with giggles. Soon, other children would begin to laugh even though they did not know the joke. Then others joined in and the laughing became contagious, moving in waves around the room. If the laughter subsided for a moment, all it would take would be one snort or one giggle and the whole class would be off again. Laughter in that moment had a life of its own.

A similar event occurred among adults on a silent retreat. Someone started giggling in the dining room. Because all of us were in silence, no one asked what was so funny; in fact, the outburst seemed like an intrusion at first. But the one who was amused could not contain her laughter, and the more she tried the funnier everything became. Soon everyone at her table was laughing, and others began to join in. Those who did not laugh out loud were smiling. The laughter mingled with the classical music, and a sense of joy and unity prevailed. Later in the evening, an elderly sister who was making a thirty-day retreat went to the leader of the group who had started the raucous behavior and whispered, "Thank you, my dear, for the gift of laughter at dinner. It softened my heart."

When we laugh together, we build relationships—we become, for the moment, sisters and brothers. We "build sympathy for one another. We become kindred spirits."[5] And, conversely, good humor and laughter depend on solid, trusting relationships. We cannot command laughter any more than we can dictate trust. We can, however, be willing to seize the funny moment, laugh out loud when least expected, find humor in our own situations, and remember Alan Watts's pronouncement: "Angels fly because they take themselves so lightly."

We can share laughter with others and discover love. We can delight in God and experience God's unconditional love for us. We can celebrate creation and witness the humor of God. These experiences lead me to wonder: Did Jesus have a sense of humor? Did Jesus laugh?

On the wall of a colleague's office hangs a large sketch of Jesus with his head thrown back, his mouth wide with laughter, his eyes sparkling. When I first saw it, I was startled and delighted. I had never thought of Jesus laughing, but when I looked at the portrait I knew it had to be true. Although we do not find the words "Jesus laughed" in the Bible, we can imagine his laughter.

Imagine laughter and joy at the wedding at Cana when the wine ran out and Jesus produced more. Imagine his rejoicing when he spoke of one child returning home, one lost sheep found, one hidden coin discovered. Imagine the humor in Jesus' eyes and the smile on his lips when he told some of his most amusing parables. Imagine what a camel would look like trying to get through the eye of a needle! If we believe Jesus to be fully human, and if we believe he cried, then I believe he must have laughed.

The laughter I imagine from Jesus is the laughter that comes from love. Yet all of laughter does not come from such a benevolent heart. We have all been hurt by the laughter that comes from mockery, being laughed at and put down. Laughter can also be confusing when we do not know what people are laughing at. I remember seeing a small child who had just done something that amused the adults around him. They began to laugh, and he began to cry. His mother comforted him saying, "But honey, it's all right, we're laughing with you." And the child wailed, "But Mommy, I'm not laughing."

My father was a humorous man, and our family life was filled with laughter. He loved to tell jokes, and he was quick with puns. He could find the delightful in many situations. My friends would say, "I love being with your family—your dad is *so* funny." And yet sometimes his jokes and humor were hurtful, because I think he was so intent on finding the humor in situations that he was not aware that his comments could wound. When I was in junior high school I was very interested in a particular boy in my algebra class. I was hoping he would invite me to a dance that was coming up. He seemed not to notice me, and then one day in the hall he smiled at me. With great excitement, I reported that smile at dinner. My father quickly retorted: "He was probably trying hard not to laugh out loud." My family laughed, because it was a funny comment, but I was devastated. My hopes were dashed, and even worse, I heard my father say I was someone who deserved to be laughed at.

When we have been hurt by laughter in the past and this wound prevents us from laughing now, we can take our hurt and our wounds to God in prayer:

> God of tears and God of laughter . . .
> Laughter has been missing in much of my life.
> I have been afraid of laughter because of
>   the many times I was ridiculed and mocked.
> Help me to know that love and laughter can go together.
> Help me to discover the joy and delight in laughter
>   shared.
> Forgive me for the times my fear has led me to laugh at
>   others.
> Forgive those who have mocked me in the past.
> Teach them and me the gift of loving laughter.

Our early experiences of laughter, humor, and joking will influence our readiness to bring laughter into our prayer lives. If we are afraid that Jesus is mocking us, we will not draw close to him. If we believe that God might laugh at us when we share our excitement and joy, we may remain silent out of fear of ridicule. But if we can learn the joy of laughter that comes from love, learning to "laugh with," find humor in human experiences, and laugh at the incongruities of creation, we may be able to learn to laugh with God.

Laughing with God

Just as tears and laughter come from the same place in the soul of humanity, might not they come from the same place in God? I have always believed in a God who weeps—who wails over injustice, who mourns with us in our grief, who cries with the lost, the imprisoned, the homeless. I believe that just as we need God's companionship in our mourning, God needs us to weep with God. No one, including God, should weep alone.

So it must be the same with laughter! When we are happy, God laughs with us. When the light shines in the darkness, God rejoices. When we delight in each other, God delights in us. I believe God wants us to laugh with God. Surely God does not wish to laugh alone.

In spiritual direction, a middle-aged divorced woman learned to laugh with God. She had been living alone for almost fifteen years when she began to make peace with her singleness, embracing it rather than fighting it. She knew from experience that life could be full and joyful without husband and children.

She found community in her local church, taking on more lay leadership. She went back to school to become more proficient in her profession. She had many friends of all backgrounds and ages. Then out of the blue she met a widower with two small daughters. She welcomed him as another friend and came to enjoy his children. Gradually their friendship turned to love, and he asked her to marry him.

She was overwhelmed, not so much by joy, but by surprise and disorientation. "How could this happen?" she sobbed to her spiritual director. "I love him, but I don't want to marry him. I don't want to be a stepmother. I like living alone. I am used to my solitude. I thought that singleness was what God had given me, and my spiritual task was to accept it. And I did. I really did. Why is God changing the plan?" Her spiritual director listened quietly and then said with a gentle smile: "Maybe this man and his children coming into your life is a sign of God's sense of humor."

The woman began to laugh, knowing what the director said was true. She had gotten so caught up with her life, her plans, her friends, and her work that she thought she was in control of her life. Her laughter was her response to the sudden and the unexpected. She did not experience God trying to trick or manipulate her. Rather, she imagined God smiling and offering her a gift and saying, "Now! What do you make of *this*?" This woman's story illustrates the words of theologian William Willimon: "The very essence of grace is to receive the gift of laughter, especially when the joke is on us."[6]

During a presentation on prayer in a local church during Lent, the congregation discovered humor in their own behavior. I had been speaking about how we have been trained to bow when invited into corporate prayer. Together we had played with other simple prayer positions such as looking forward with our eyes open, then looking upward with eyes on the cross. We discussed many other issues about prayer before I brought the evening to an end. I thanked them for coming and being such enthusiastic participants, and then I said: "Shall we end in prayer?" Like magic, all their heads went down. So I added, "And you need not bow your heads." Great laughter followed—a shared laughter of recognition, a gentle humor about ourselves. So I looked up as I led the closing prayer. The congregation placed their bodies in positions of their choice. And we were still smiling when we said, "Amen." It was wonderful for all of us to experience communal laughter in church.

Merriment in Church

In *A Passage to India*, E. M. Forster describes a hilarious Hindu worship service in which practical jokes are played on people. Many participants take turns at being the clown or the fool. Their words are funny, their actions absurd, and everyone is having a grand time honoring the presence of God. He writes:

> By sacrificing good taste, this worship achieved what Christianity has shirked: the inclusion of merriment. All spirit as well as all matter must participate in salvation, and if practical jokes are banned, the circle is incomplete.[7]

Christianity did not always shirk merriment and hilarity. From the twelfth century to the sixteenth century, the church celebrated the Feast of Fools. The key to this festival was reversal. The high were brought low, the lowly were exalted, the serious were mocked, and liturgical rituals overturned. Harvard professor Harvey Cox, in his book *The Feast of Fools*, describes it this way:

> Ordinarily pious priests and serious townsfolk donned bawdy masks, sang outrageous ditties, and generally kept the whole world awake with revelry and satire. Minor clerics painted their faces, strutted about in the robes of their superiors, and mocked the stately rituals of church and court. Sometimes a Lord of Misrule, a Mock King, or a Boy Bishop was elected to preside over the events. In some places the Boy Bishop even celebrated a parody mass. During the Feast of Fools, no custom or convention was immune to ridicule and even the highest personages of the realm could expect to be lampooned.[8]

Not everyone experienced the Feast of Fools as fun. Occasionally the revelry went too far and violence broke out. People were injured and property destroyed. Those of the highest rank did not appreciate being brought low, even for a day. And the hierarchy, who believed that their solemn rituals were the only way to God, denounced any idea of bringing fun and play into the worship of God. The Feast was condemned by the Council of Basel in 1431, but survived in a variety of forms until the sixteenth century. In the age of Reformation, it slowly died out in response to the rising value of the qualities of sobriety, thrift, industry, and ambition.[9]

Without bringing back the Feast of Fools, how might we incorporate some of the elements of the Feast into our worship of God? We need to extract the spirit of play, the reversals, the paradox, and the new vision that comes from turning the world "upside down." Play and laughter break open the rigid, expand the narrow, and nudge us out of our ruts. Play and laughter lead to new possibilities in our relationship with God and in our relationships with our sisters and brothers.

In biblical times, Sarah brought her community together with laughter, and Jesus brought his community together with amusing stories, unusual images, and paradox. In medieval times the Feast of Fools brought people together with a festival of play and role reversal. Today our communities could become willing to open to the absurd, the playful, the fun, and the funny. We could discover a new way of being together and a deeper connection through the simple act of laughing together. Laughter can be sacred. Laughter participates in God.

In an attempt to bring merriment into worship, many pastors include a joke or an amusing tale in their sermons. These stories often bring a chuckle from the congregation, but rarely do they elicit pure laughter. Laughter comes from the unexpected, the double entendre, the situation that no one expected. Children in church are often the source of laughter, because they pipe up with whatever they are thinking in the moment. Any Christian educator knows that a Pandora's box is opened when youngsters are asked an open-ended question during the children's sermon.

A more structured way of bringing the playful, the absurd, the laughter into our churches is through clown ministries. The purpose of clowns is to "restore the balance of work and play, reverence and irreverence. They want to affirm the need to be serious at times without being solemn; to be respectful without being idolatrous; and to be religious without being judgmental."[10]

Christian clowns come in many forms with a variety of functions. Liturgical clowns bring humor and play and creativity into worship and seek "to deepen the congregation's experience through the use of laughter."[11] A clown might follow the procession into church and then pop up at unexpected moments to encourage the congregation to respond to the hymns, or the sermon, or the prayers. A clown might mime a particular Bible verse or sermon illustration. The liturgical clown does not distract us from the worship of God, but rather draws us more deeply into the worship experience.

Pastoral clowns are also healers. They reach out to the ill and lonely and frightened in new ways. A clown in the children's ward of a hospital brings smiles of delight to patients and staff. A clown visiting a nursing home reminds the residents of their youth and in nonverbal ways allows them to connect in fun to another human being. Imagine what it might be like if a pastor took a clown with her when she visited a homebound parishioner. Shifting a usual visit into one of fun and nonverbal exchange might ease in a new way the day-to-day loneliness of the one who is alone.

Social action clowns address the pressing issues of the day by presenting new ways of seeing old situations. They do not attempt to present what is right or what is wrong. Rather, they place the situation in a new light and open up a new vision. "Clowns dare to juggle all into the air and let it fall again in a new conclusion."[12]

In many ways, all of us are clowns. We do not need training or grease paint or an audience to play the fool. All we need to do is recognize the absurdities of life, the incongruities of interactions, the possibilities on the other side of convention. We need to be willing to laugh at ourselves and our situations, play tag with a humorous God, and allow our faces to break into smiles at inappropriate moments. When we come to a place in our prayer life where we are able to "let go and let God," our surrender may be welcomed with great bursts of heavenly laughter as we fall joyfully into the playful presence of God.

ACTIVITIES FOR REFLECTION AND DISCUSSION

1. Carry with you a small notebook in which to jot down the things you find in your days that make you laugh, that delight you, or that you find humorous. Look around yourself and at yourself for the amusing, the comical, and the absurd. Think of this task as a treasure hunt for the humorous in your life. Share your list with a friend or with a group, helping each other see the funny side of people and events that surround us. Fashion a prayer of words or movements or symbols to share your delight and your laughter with God.

2. In the beginning of this chapter I imagined playing hide and seek with God. What would it mean to play other games with God? What about tag? Can you imagine chasing God until you got so close you could cry, "You're it!"? And then run away with God chasing you until you are caught? Imagine "Ring Around the Rosie," or "Mother May I?" or "Red Rover, Red Rover," or "Musical Chairs." What about less structured games, games of fantasy and spontaneity and "let's pretend"? Begin looking for opportunities that arise in your daily life to play with God. If you are part of a discussion group, find ways that you could play together with God, and discover how play could become part of your corporate prayer.

3. If you have been hurt by laughter in the past, and this prevents you from laughing now, write a prayer that speaks to God about your special needs. As you fashion your own prayer, be specific about the hurts that you

have experienced and the memories that still hurt. Be willing to ask for what you need to heal these hurts. Imagine the places in your life where you would love to receive the gift of laughter. Pour out your hurts and your longings to God, who will not scorn or mock or belittle you. Be assured that God will not laugh at you.

4. William Willimon wrote: "Among all God's creatures, human beings are the only animals who both laugh and weep—for we are the only animals who are struck with the difference between the way things are and the way things ought to be.[13] When does seeing the "ought to be" make you laugh? When does it make you weep? Think of specific examples and share them in your discussion group. Notice how everyone may not have the same response to a particular situation. Reflect together about what situations in our world today may make God laugh and which situations may make God weep.

5

~e~~9~

PRAYING WITH
OUR IMAGINATIONS

"The soul without imagination is what an observatory would be without a telescope," wrote the Reverend H.W. Beecher, father of Harriet Beecher Stowe. Therefore, if we are to pray with body and soul we must include the imagination, because without it our prayers might be beautifully structured but they would be empty and purposeless.

The imagination is defined as the "formation of mental images of objects not present to the senses, especially of those never perceived in their entirety; hence mental synthesis of new ideas from elements experienced separately."[1] To bring this definition into our lived experience, I will guide you on a brief journey down memory lane.

> Think for a moment about a place you lived when you were growing up. Remember the rooms, the door that was used most often, the feel of the floors, the special places you enjoyed. Remember living there. Place yourself where you slept and played and studied and ate. Remember the people who lived with you.

If these words brought memories of sights, sounds, and smells to your mind and heart, you have just fulfilled the first part of the definition of imagination: "The formation of mental images or objects not present to the senses." To complete the definition of imagination, add yourself as an adult to the memory of your childhood home:

> Close your eyes and imagine yourself returning to the place of your childhood with all the new knowledge of yourself and the world that you have gained since you left. Walk through the door and through the rooms, seeing this place from a new perspective. What do you see? Does anything surprise you? What feelings are evoked? Are there words you wish to speak to anyone there?

If you were in any way able to experience your childhood home from the perspective of an adult, you have just created a "mental synthesis of new ideas from elements experienced separately." Your imagination is alive and well!

Like the observatory needs the telescope, the soul needs the imagination. Without an imagination, the soul would have no way of communicating with us, no way to pull our attention to its needs, no way to tell us how deeply we are connected to God. The soul also needs the imagination to let us know of its very existence, because no one has ever seen the soul, heard the soul, touched, tasted, or smelled the soul. We cannot know the soul through our senses. We cannot describe the soul in any logical, concrete way, but the imaginations of people across the ages have painted word pictures of the soul:

> "God has made the soul so cunningly
> and so secretly that no one knows
> truly what she is."[2]

> In a hand like a bowl,
> Danced my own soul,
> Small as an elf,
> All by itself.[3]

"We know our soul by its acts, its thought patterns, its reverie, by the quality of its attention . . . "[4]

In a dance class, after an extended period of movement designed to connect the dancers to their souls, the participants were invited to share images. Some of the words for soul were "weaver," "bit of the Great Spirit," "witnesses," "radiant jewel." One woman added, "To me my soul is my own personal cheerleader!"

Exercising the Imagination

W. Somerset Maugham wrote that "imagination grows by exercise, and contrary to common belief, is more powerful in the mature than in the young." To experience this power and learn to pray with body and soul, some of us need to bring our imaginations out of retirement and allow them to become more active in our lives. We exercise our imaginations every time we read or hear or tell a story. We exercise our imaginations when we plan for upcoming events such as a child's homecoming, or a gathering of close friends, or an important business meeting, or a visit to the homeless shelter to serve a meal. Our imaginations are getting fine workouts when we wish and dream and hope. Our imaginations are part of laughing and playing with God.

A less familiar way of exercising our imaginations is to attend to the images with which we surround ourselves. Images activate our imaginations and invite them into our daily lives. I am very intentional about the images that surround me in my office where I work, study, write, and pray. I have selected them for the purpose of keeping my imagination awake, my heart open, and my mind centered on God.

A copy of Rembrandt's "The Return of the Prodigal Son" stands on the end table facing a comfortable chair. A seated Buddha radiates peace from the corner of my desk. Next to him is a small turtle with turquoise eyes reminding me of the slow process of transformation, while a finely carved snow leopard radiates the movement and grace of the spirit. Many symbols adorn my bookshelves: a tiny ivory madonna that belonged to my grand-mother, a pottery bowl that contains dirt from the Sanctuary of Chimayo, an icon of Jesus the Liberator, a ring brought to me from the 1996 Women's Conference in Beijing, and a tiny replica of the God Krishna carved inside a walnut shell. A beautiful blank book that my sister brought to me from a Peruvian marketplace rests by my elbow, awaiting prayers and dreams. On another wall is an ordination gift—a framed crocheted butterfly with the words from 2 Corinthians 5:17 written beneath: "Behold all things are become new." A small stuffed bear sits on a low footstool, and under the table rests another stuffed animal, Priscilla the Goose. My mother's cane leans in the corner.

I have gathered these symbols and images around me to nurture my imagination and to speak to my soul. Once in a while, I move the images about, finding them new resting places, or grouping them in different ways. Occasionally I retire an image when it no longer holds meaning for me. A new symbol might catch my heart and I add it to the wall, or the shelves, or the desk. I change my icons regularly, allowing different images of the Christ to grace my room.

While playing with images opens our hearts to the nonverbal imagina-tion, we can also exercise our imaginations through language. Words evok-ing imagination are one of the many blessings of the Bible. As you read the following passages, allow the words to guide your imagination so that you are seeing and hearing, feeling and touching, tasting, and smelling the expe-riences described:

> For you shall go out in joy,
>   and be led back in peace;
> the mountains and the hills before you
>   shall burst into song,
>   and all the trees of the field shall clap their hands.
> (Isa. 55:12)

> Oh, may your breasts be like clusters of the vine,
>   and the scent of your breath like apples,
>   and your kisses like the best wine
>   that goes down smoothly,
>   gliding over lips and teeth.
> (Song of Songs 7:8-9)

Six days later, Jesus took with him Peter and James and John, and led them up a high mountain apart, by themselves. And he was transfigured before them, and his clothes became dazzling white, such as no one on earth could bleach them. (Mark 9:2-3)

And they clothed him in a purple cloak; and after twisting some thorns into a crown, they put it on him. And they began saluting him, "Hail, King of the Jews!" They struck his head with a reed, spat upon him, and knelt down in homage to him. (Mark 15:17-19)

When we read the Bible with our imaginations receptive and alive, we hear the words and understand the message at new and deeper levels. The imagination allows all of who we are to become involved in Bible reading. But we do not need to stop with our heightened awareness of the words and the stories; we can allow our imaginations to guide us into prayer.

Prayer and the Imagination

Using the imagination to enter into Bible stories to discover new ways to pray is not a modern-day phenomenon. In the sixteenth century St. Ignatius of Loyola, the founder of the Jesuit Order, taught in his Spiritual Exercises how to imaginatively enter the Gospel stories to be transformed by the Word of God. A student reported the following experience after reading the work of St. Ignatius:

> I was meditating upon the Bible passage where Pilate is in front of the angry crowd and the crowd is demanding that Jesus be crucified. As I finished reading this narrative, I began to imagine myself "in the story." I repeated the words of the passage again in my mind. I tried to see pictures, but they were not coming to me. About the time I decided to give up on this meditation, I suddenly "heard" huge footsteps coming down a great stone hallway. Immediately I was transported into the story.
>
> In my mind's eye I looked around. I was in a great hallway in the residence of Pilate. Coming down the hall were soldiers who were leading the condemned Jesus toward crucifixion. As I saw them coming I slipped into a room off the hall so I would not be noticed by the guards. My heart pounded as I heard the group go by. When I sensed they had passed, I

looked out the doorway. I watched Jesus slip away from the group and come toward me, gently pushing me back into the room.

Jesus had been badly beaten. He was bruised and blood ran down his face. I said to him, "I can't believe they are doing this to you. You shouldn't have to die. I am so sorry." Jesus looked into my eyes and said, "Do not be sorry. Simply look at me and see me as I really am." At once Jesus was transformed into a perfect being. All his cuts and bruises were gone. His face shone with a glory I can hardly describe. "Know that I love you and this is something I must now do," he said while looking deeply into my eyes. He turned and was gone as suddenly as he had appeared.

Using the imagination to enter a Bible story can be done alone as this student did, or it can be done in a group. Many people's imaginations going to work on one passage can add to the creativity of entering Bible stories, because your ideas and images will stimulate and build on other people's imaginations. A group of students reading Luke 6:17-19 together used their imaginations to create a living, breathing, noisy setting in which they placed themselves to discover what this particular healing story could teach them about prayer. Luke 6:17 places Jesus and the recently chosen twelve apostles in a clearing after a night of prayer on the mountain:

> He came down with them and stood on a level place, with a great crowd of his disciples and a great multitude of people from all Judea, Jerusalem, and the coast of Tyre and Sidon. They had come to hear him and to be healed of their diseases; and those who were troubled with unclean spirits were cured, and all in the crowd were trying to touch him, for the power came out from him and healed them all. (Luke 6:17-19)

The students were asked many questions and their imaginations responded:

> How many people do you imagine were there? "Hundreds." "Thousands." "Like a rock concert." "Like all the people who gather to see a famous person."
>
> What people do you imagine were there? "The old and the sick." "Families, people alone." "Children, babies, people carried to Jesus for healing." "The scoffers, the curious, the believers." "People there by accident on the way to somewhere else."
>
> What would it sound like, feel like, smell like? "People shouting, crowds pushing." "The smells of food and of illness, of unwashed bodies and sweat." "Hot and dusty, a wind blowing debris around." "Some people may have been waiting for days." "The crowd would be filled with anticipation, frustration, fear, hope, worry, concern."

As the students talked and added their ideas and images, these three verses of the Bible became a roiling, teeming, colorful event filled with movement and sounds and smells. They began to imagine and express what it would have been like to be part of the crowd:

> "I'm too *short*. I can't see!" "I'm rudely pushing myself forward." "I'm staying on the edge. I don't want to get too close." "I'm so afraid that Jesus won't see me." "I wish I hadn't come."

As the picture became full, and they had placed themselves in the biblical event, I read the last verse: " . . . for power came out from him and healed all of them." The students remained quiet, experiencing the healing in their imaginations. "All of them. All of us!" one of them breathed. Then, using their imaginations, the other students continued the story:

> "I imagine the crowd got quiet like we did." "Some people didn't know what had happened." "Maybe some won't know for years." "I think the people left quietly." "I imagine they praised God." "Jesus said and did nothing, and all of the people were healed." "What a wonderful example of true presence." "I can just begin to imagine the power and the love that was in that place."

The students left class with the invitation to respond to their experience with a drawing, an image of their own making to remind them and guide them in their prayer. They discovered that their drawings kept their imaginations alive, providing no easy answers but rather a number of questions that guided them even more deeply into the healing miracle. Some related they were reminded of times of healing in their own lives, and others began to notice places in their own lives in need of healing. All of them said that reading these Bible verses with their imaginations had affected their understanding of the passage and had led them to new ways of prayer. Some were called to prayers of praise, others to prayers for healing. One woman said that drawing her picture was her prayer. Another was pulled to quiet contemplation, simply resting in the loving presence of Jesus.

Wendy Wright, teacher and author, has said that "the extraordinary thing about the imagination is that it enables us to have access to what is not readily observable."[5] This statement feels to me like a description of prayer. Because prayer is our response to God's call to relationship, the imagination is that which allows us to both hear the call and respond to the call. The imagination also helps us receive the effects of prayer.

A young man called me in great distress. He was confused and despairing and had many physical challenges. He knew people were praying for him, but he could not "feel" their prayers. I asked him what prayers "felt" like. "I don't know, I don't know. I only know I am feeling nothing." "What is a comforting experience for you?" I asked him. "What action on the part of another brings comfort to your body and soul?" "When I was a child and not feeling well," he remembered, "I would lie on the couch watching television. If I fell asleep, my mother or my father would gently cover me with a blanket." I suggested, "When you lie down tonight, imagine the prayers of all your friends covering you gently with a blanket of their care and love. Use your imagination to feel their prayers."

We of the Western world tend to be so concrete and rational. I can hear questions arising from this story. Isn't the young man just fooling himself? Is he imagining himself into a desired feeling? What if no one is praying for him? I understand the purpose of prayer is to deepen our relationships with God and with others. If the young man's pain is eased by his imagining the people in his life who care about him, is that not a prayer received? If he falls asleep under an imagined blanket of love, is that any less real than the love he received from his parents and the love God pours out on him? In this instance his imagination is not creating that which is not there. Rather, his imagination gives him access to what truly is.[6]

Sometimes the fruits of our imagination can be a gift to another person. In a group spiritual-direction session, a participant on retreat shared issues of loneliness, a heaviness of heart, a longing for God in the midst of difficulties. As one of the four directors needing to respond to the man's story, I wrestled with an image that was very strong, but I was not sure that my image was an appropriate response. I imagined his heart being pierced. Because I had nothing else to say, and the image was so vivid, I shared it with him. He was puzzled and said it did not resonate with his experience, but he would hold it in the spirit of love with which it was offered.

Two weeks later I received a letter from him telling me that after the retreat he had recalled the lyrics of the Bob Dylan song "If You See Her, Say Hello," from the album *Blood on the Tracks*. Dylan's words related how the separation from his lover was so painful that it pierced his heart, but because of their love they were never truly apart. She was inside him forever.

He went on to say: "As with many love songs the Beloved (Divine) can easily be substituted for the beloved (woman), which is why these words have such deep meaning for me. This is the first time I can recall receiving such a clear message in this manner, and I was greatly affected by it. It really came as a direct answer to my question, 'How do I find God in my heart?'" I left the retreat filled with feelings of joy and vitality and love."

Another way to engage the imagination in prayer is to create for yourself in your mind and heart your special place to pray. Think for a moment when and where you are most comfortable at prayer, when prayer is as natural as breathing and there is nothing interfering with your longing to be with God.

Create or recreate this place in your imagination, using all your senses to experience your own sacred place. When you are satisfied with your imaginary place, picture yourself going there to pray. Do you fall to your knees, do you dance, do you sing? Watch yourself at prayer, freely responding to God's invitation to relationship. Complete your prayer in your imagination and ask yourself, "Was I imagining I was praying, or was I praying?"

A personal, sacred space in the imagination helps us make the transition from our active, busy, linear lives to an attentive attitude of asking, responding, praising God. Go to your spot whenever you feel the need of prayer. I imagine you will discover how easy prayer can be and will see how the holy can be close to you every minute of the day and night.

Prayer Pictures

Colors, lines, and shapes give form to our imaginations and are a powerful way to pray. As the students drew their response to the healing story in Luke, so can you put to paper or model in clay your prayerful response to a Bible passage, personal encounter, a disturbing incident, a constant anxiety, a celebration. Often we do not pray because we do not know what to say. But if we were relieved of words by picking up our crayons or our markers or our lump of clay, we might find ourselves praying more frequently, more readily, more easily.

"But what will I draw?" you ask. See if you are willing to simply begin with any color and move your hand across the paper. When you feel finished with that color, pick up another. Hold an attitude of nonjudgment and a willingness to be surprised. Play with lines and shapes, the flat side of the crayon as well as the point. Draw and color until you feel finished, and then sit with your creation, suspending analysis. Gaze at the paper with soft eyes and see if it speaks to you about your relationship with God.

When people are unable to suspend judgment and try hard to draw"something," which usually turns out not looking like "anything," I recommend that they draw with their nondominant hand. This does two things. First, it gives a good excuse for the drawing being so unrecognizable and it brings in an element of play! Second, when we draw with our nondominant hand, we contact the child within and we tend to draw and pray as simply and as easily as children. Jesus did invite us to come to him as little children. By praying in this way we are honoring his request.

Drawing prayers is a wonderful way to involve children in praying. Children don't usually ask what to draw or how to draw. When their hearts are full, they just begin drawing with an eagerness that we might learn from.

If a loved one is in the hospital and is in need of prayers, ask children to draw their "get well prayers" for a friend. When times of joy are at hand, ask children to draw their prayers of thanksgiving and gratitude. When a child is hurting, upset, or angry, ask her to draw a picture for God expressing what is in her body and soul. A mother told me how her children, who had enjoyed this form of prayer when they were younger, had continued it into their adolescence. At a difficult and trying time in her life when she was looking desperately for employment, her three children handed her their prayer drawings as she headed out the door for an important interview. "Here are our prayers for your success, Mom. Good luck!"

Nothing helps children pray more than a parent or loved adult praying with them. So join your children in this practice. If you have no children, join your inner child and draw your prayers to God. Nothing is more disruptive to this prayer practice than judgment or analysis. Even if you are able to suspend judgment, the desire to probe, question, and understand is sometimes too much for us. But we must resist the temptation and simply witness the image and allow the child to understand her drawing in her own way and her own time. I share with you a story of how adult judgment and analysis can miss the creative wisdom of the child.

A small boy in kindergarten discovered paints. He spent all his free time at the easel. He learned to mix the colors and use wide brush strokes. Sometimes he painted in fine lines. His teachers and parents were excited by his gift and hung his pictures around the room. He never offered an explanation of his artwork, and the adults never asked. The paintings were simply a beautiful expression of life rendered by a child.

One day when he had completed a particularly colorful painting, he stood back admiring it and then picked up his brush, filled it with black paint, and slowly and carefully covered his painting. All the colors were obliterated; nothing was left except the black. His teacher thought this odd, but was not alarmed until the boy began to end all of his painting sessions in this manner.

His parents were called. "Is everything all right at home?" The teacher sent him to the school psychologist. They began watching and documenting his behavior. Covering his beautiful paintings with black *must* indicate something wrong. It was not normal. What could be the matter? The boy himself behaved no differently in other areas of his life and was unaware of all the fuss he was creating.

One day, a young student teacher stood behind him as he completed his painting and carefully prepared his black brush. "Why do you cover your painting with black?" she asked him casually. He beamed up at her, seemingly pleased that someone had finally asked. "Because life is like a play," he responded. "And at the end of every act, the curtain comes down!"

Praying with Dream Images

Dreams are the form the imagination takes when we are asleep. The study of dreams, the interpretation of dreams, and the fascination with dreams are not only modern phenomena. Joseph, son of Jacob, was a well-known dreamer in Hebrew Scripture. As a young man, Joseph dreamed of greatness (Gen. 37:1-11). When he told his brothers of his dreams they became jealous. The brothers schemed to get rid of Joseph and they found a way to sell him as a slave. Joseph ended up in Egypt, where he became an interpreter of dreams, winning his freedom and subsequently rising to power by his vivid interpretation of Pharaoh's dream (Gen. 42).

His namesake, Joseph, husband of Mary, was also guided by dreams. His decision to dismiss Mary quietly when he found she was with child was changed when an angel of the Lord appeared to him in a dream (Matt. 1:18-20). In a second dream, Joseph was told by the angel of the Lord to flee with Jesus and Mary into Egypt, where they would be safe from Herod's proclamation to kill all the young children around Bethlehem (Matt. 2:13-15).

In addition to these specific dreamers, the Bible records or mentions dreams or similar experiences from Genesis to Revelation. The early church continued the interest in dreams and dreaming. "Every major figure of the early Christian Church through the time of St. Augustine cites dreams as an important way in which God spoke to humankind."[7]

In modern times, psychologists, psychiatrists, and medical researchers have become attentive to dreams and dreaming. Laboratory studies have researched the physiological components of dreaming. Sigmund Freud and Carl Jung began paying attention to patients' dreams, finding in them images that could lead to healing. Today many psychologists help clients understand their dreams. There are dream groups where people share and discuss their dreams. Self-help books on dream interpretations are available, and people bring up their dreams in casual conversations.

Today dreams are also experienced through religious and spiritual lenses. Dreams may contain religious images and symbols that might indicate their spiritual nature. Sometimes dreams are interpreted as messages from God. Sometimes a dream seems to call for a spiritual or religious response.

For example, a woman had a vivid dream of a friend she had not seen in years. In the dream, she and her friend were walking arm-in-arm down a beautiful garden path. No words were spoken, but the dream held a promise of intimacy. When she awoke, she was close to tears, because this friend and she had had a series of disagreements years before and the conflict had never been resolved. She realized it was time to let go of her hurt and jealousy and righteous anger and move toward reconciliation and forgiveness.

In another case a young man dreamed of himself as a child playing with many friends on an elaborate wooden jungle gym. In the midst of their play, the whole structure collapsed around them. He felt great fear as beams and poles crashed to the ground. Then he realized that he stood in the midst of the rubble without a scratch and all the other children were skipping away. He felt the dream was telling him that it was all right to let go of his old structures of belief that no longer had meaning for him. It was frightening to stand alone with the opportunity to rebuild, but he recognized that neither he nor anyone else was hurt in the dismantling of his old systems of religious thought.

When I was thinking about going to seminary, I had the following dream:

> I am in New York City. I have a story to tell. I stop at a large and busy intersection. People gather around me in a circle. They are stern, but not judging. Listening. I begin with confidence. I am standing in the center of the crossed streets. Because of interruptions I am not allowed to finish.

When I awoke, I realize I had been speaking from the center of a circle at the center of the cross.

This and other dreams influenced my call to ministry and I wrote my ordination paper with the title "Guided by Dreams."[8] I continue to be interested in the ways dreams might guide us by pointing out options, reassuring us of progress, and helping us with choices. But I have added a new way to approach dreams. The question I am most likely to ask now is: "How might our dreams teach us to pray?" I have come to believe that a dream may be an invitation to prayer.

For years I have had a series of anxiety dreams. They usually occur before some public presentation—a lecture, a book reading, a sermon, a retreat. The specific details are different but the theme is always the same: I cannot get anyone to listen to me. People won't sit down. Or they start moving chairs as I begin to speak. One time, they all left the room to go to the kitchen to mix a huge tossed salad. Another time, the place where the audience was sitting turned into a boat and sailed away, leaving me behind. I have come to accept these dreams and often find them amusing, but only recently have I allowed them to guide me into prayer.

Now when I have an anxiety dream, I am reminded that if I am to effectively communicate whatever I am trying to say, I need God's help. Often in the preparation for a public appearance I get caught up in my importance, or my own words, or how I will be received. I forget that what I am doing is part of my ministry and I am doing it for God, not for success. These reminders lead me to prayers for humility, for guidance, to be open to the Spirit so I can be guided in my speaking. My prayers help me to return to what is important and help me to release my ego attachment to my "performance."

I try to listen to the dreams of others with the same question in mind: "How might this dream guide you in prayer?" When a directee told me she had had a dream that she could not remember except that she awoke with the refrain of a favorite hymn from childhood echoing in her heart, we talked about the dream as a prayer and about her willingness to use that refrain as part of daily prayer. The words she remembered were: "He walks with me and he talks with me and he tells me I am his own." This became a simple and profound prayer to remind her of God's continual presence in her life.

Another directee had a disturbing dream in which three stones were removed from her breast. In the way of dreams, there was no surgery, no blood, they were simply lifted away. She was frightened about what this could mean. We talked about the breast as another name for the heart and I wondered if the image could mean that a heaviness, a burden had been removed from her heart. She had recently been relating a story from years ago that she had always held secret. She had been worried if the telling was appropriate. "Telling the story *has* been freeing," she said. "I have told the truth and God has lifted the heaviness from my heart." We talked how this realization might lead her in prayer. "Thanksgiving!" she exclaimed. "I want and need to pray my gratitude."

A woman on retreat reported her dream:

> I was sitting on a stage with the district attorney from a neighboring county. He was stern and rigid and judgmental and I was afraid of him. But when the meeting was over I spontaneously put my arms around him and said: "God bless you." He crumbled and wept in my arms.

The other retreatants were silent as they imagined this powerful transformation. Then one retreatant spoke: "I wonder if you are to ask God's blessing on all the judgmental and controlling parts of yourself?" With gentle guidance, the retreatant discovered a new way to pray for herself.

Dreams may not always point us to specific forms of prayer but may give us an image to rest with. A man dreamed he was holding a small animal and stroking it lovingly. He found great pleasure imaging that he was the animal and God was stroking him lovingly. "A comforting image when I am not feeling very lovable," he said.

A woman dreamed that on the other side of a door on which she had knocked was a herd of alert and peaceful deer. This image reminded her of the biblical teaching, "Knock, and the door will be opened for you" (Luke

11:9). The dream image gave her encouragement to keep praying, knowing that peace awaited her.

I recently had a dream in which a loud voice woke me up saying: "Faith is the will of God." I was very disoriented, because my dreams usually come in visual images. But I felt compelled to write the dream down. I found a scrap of paper and wrote the words, stumbled back to bed and into a sound sleep. The next morning my husband asked me if the illegible note on his desk was for him, and only when I read it did I recall the dream.

I asked my spiritual director about it and she said it sounded like the messages the Ammas and Abbas of the desert gave to people who asked them questions. "These holy people," she told me, "would often respond in riddles that would short-circuit logical thinking. Sometimes their advice seemed foolish, such as, 'Plant this dead stick and water it faithfully. Watch it carefully.'" She told me my phrase sounded like a riddle and instead of trying to figure it out I should "water it and see what grows." I am still "watering," watching, waiting, and wondering. But her advice was wise, because when I recall and repeat the phrase I am comforted by the mysterious message.

You do not need to know anything about dream interpretation to allow your dreams to guide you in prayer, and more deeply into your relationship with God. You don't even need to remember the specifics about a dream. Just stay connected to the feelings the dream evoked, and maybe to an image, if you can remember one. Then ask yourself the question: "How might this dream guide my prayer?" Hold the question lightly, do not struggle for an answer, and allow your imagination to guide you to a prayerful response.

Images of God

> But Moses said to God, "If I come to the Israelites and say to them, 'The God of your ancestors has sent me to you,' and they ask me, 'What is his name?' What shall I say to them?" God said to Moses, "I AM WHO I AM." (Exod. 3:13-14a)

Moses and God are discussing theology—which may be as profoundly simple as the naming of God and struggling with all that a name implies. God's words, "I AM WHO I AM," provide Moses with a message for the Israelites but leaves us to name for ourselves the great I AM. Naming God for ourselves requires an active imagination as well as analytical thought. Only the imagination can glimpse the full mystery of God. Only the imagination can name God.

Our images and our names for God are a way we do theology. Theology does not have to be only well studied, abstract, intellectual ideas. True theology may be as immediate, as grounded, as intuitive as prayer. Roberta Bondi, teacher and author, says that "prayer and theological reflection vitally need each other; they are two parts of a whole that cannot be separated."[9]

We have been doing theology throughout this book, although this is the first time we are using that term. I have been making assumptions about God, and you have either accepted my assumptions or have argued with them or have opened up your own assumptions to make room for mine. When we talk about praying with our senses, we assume that God can be known through the created world. When we understand the deep connection between sexuality and spirituality and that God calls us to deep intimacy, we assume a God of unconditional love. When we pray to God for healing, we assume a God of compassion. When we know that laughter can be a prayer, we assume a God with a sense of humor. All statements about prayer are theological pronouncements. "Every bit of praying each of us ever does, whether in words, gestures, attitudes, or emotions, is always grounded in who we at least unconsciously think God is."[10]

Just as all our prayers reveal our theology, so our theology will determine how we pray. If we believe God to be a mighty judge, we will make sure our prayers are well-worded and appropriate so that God will be pleased. If we question God's trustworthiness, we will be always watchful in prayer, holding back that which we feel might be misunderstood. If we think of God as a theological construct, we will not pray with words of love and intimacy, because who can get close to an abstraction? If we believe God to be watching humankind but not involved in the unfolding of events, it makes no sense to pray prayers of petition or intercession. If we believe God to be unconditional love, we will pray whatever comes to mind and heart, body and soul, assured of total acceptance.

We may not be clear in our theological thinking. We may not know who God is. We may have given up one image of God but have not yet replaced it with another. We may be trying to work out our own theology. But not being totally clear about God need not keep us from prayer. While we think and sort and wrestle with who God is, we can accept the mystery of God. We can also use a variety of names for God, names that do not define or constrict God, but rather make the glorious mystery of God more accessible. One way to play with this idea is to find new and different ways to address God and see what prayers follow. A variety of names for God will lead to diversity in prayers.

On a prayer retreat I invited the participants to write very brief prayers after I had given them a particular name for God. I asked them to be open to what might be called forth by beginning prayers in different ways. They were amazed at the richness of the prayers they wrote and were willing to share them with each other. We had a profound prayer circle as each person picked an original prayer to pray aloud.

Comforting, Compassionate God: You have made yourself known to me in difficult times. You have helped me through much pain and sorrow. You have let me know that I need not walk alone.

God of stillness: Hear me! Answer me!

God of the stillness: Listen to your child and bring peace into my chaotic day.

O God who seeks for me: Here I am!

Weaver/spinner God: This is a tangled transition of life. I trust that I might find the right connection and path. I trust that you will lead me.

Weaver/spinner God: Unravel the knots in my daily existence and help me put my life back into an even pattern of love and accord.

Dear Mystery: Although we may never completely comprehend you, on occasion we taste your sweetness.

Furious Mother Bear God: I am angry and need help finding a way through.

Grandmother God: Who loves me unconditionally and always has time to listen, hold me again in the security of your lap and rock me in your peace.

Dear Grandmother God: Help me to understand my heritage and then lead me in teaching those in my care.

O God, my rock and my salvation: Give me solid footing in you.

AMEN!

ACTIVITIES FOR REFLECTION AND DISCUSSION

1. Make an inventory of the images that surround you. Decide which ones you want to remain with you. Decide which ones you want to retire. Think also whether there is an image you would like to include in your surroundings, such as a clown to remind you of the humorous side of life, or a small shell to remind you of the depth of the sea, or a glass prism that will

throw rainbows on your wall, or a dream catcher to help you remember your dreams. Each member of a discussion group might bring to a meeting one image that is particularly important to him or her. Sharing images with one another helps us to know each other on a deeper level. Sharing images also opens up new paths to God.

2. Read the story of Jesus blessing the little children in Luke 18:15-17. Use your imagination to make the setting of this story live and breathe. Where is Jesus? Is he sitting or standing? Who are the people who are bringing the children to him? Are they in line, or pushing their way into Jesus' presence? What is the age range of the children being brought to Jesus? How do they react to Jesus and to the other children and to the adults standing around? Imagine the disapproval of the disciples and hear their stern words. What do they do when Jesus rebukes them? How would you feel if you were there as a child or if you were bringing your child to Jesus? What would you like to say to Jesus? How do you imagine him responding? As you come away from Jesus, what would be your prayer?

3. Buy a box of crayons or colored pencils and a blank notebook. Become familiar with your colors by simply using them on the paper. Play with drawing with your nondominant hand. Do not try to create anything; simply notice the colors and how you mark your paper. When you feel ready, open your Bible to Romans 5:1-5, which is a brief but complex passage about Paul's understanding of justification by faith, and the grace that we receive as a result of our faith. Read through the passage without analyzing it or trying to figure out exactly what it means. Then let one or two verses grab your attention, letting go of other verses that do not interest you or connect to your experience. Read the verses or phrases you have selected over again. Read them slowly. Read them out loud. Now take your crayons or your clay and draw or shape a response to the words. When you have finished, gaze at your drawing or your sculpture with soft eyes, letting your images speak to you about faith and grace and God's loving presence in your life.

4. Remember a dream you have had recently. Write it down in as much detail as you can. Pay attention to how this dream makes you feel. Reflect on associations you have with images from the dream. Hold the dream and the experience of the dream lightly, asking not what the dream means, but how it might guide you in prayer. If you are reading and praying with a group, you might share your dream and see if someone else might hear in your dream any indications of new ways to pray.

5. Write brief prayers for these different names for God. See if you are willing to allow each address to pull a new unexpected prayer from your heart.

Source of all life:
Jesus, my brother:
God of the potter's wheel:
God of the whirlwind:
Gentle shepherd:
Grandfather God:
Great spirit:
Lamb of God:

Are there other names for God which are particularly appropriate for you right now in your life? Write these names as well and allow them to lead you into prayer.

6

OUR MANY SELVES
GUIDE US IN PRAYER

We call God by many names. Created in God's image, we too have many names. For example, I am Reverend Vennard when people are formal. I am Jane to most people. A few friends call me Janie. My husband has affectionate nicknames for me. And for a period of my youth I tried to get people to call me by my middle name, Elizabeth. When I was teaching fourth grade, some of my students called me Teacher, as a few students now call me Professor. I am one person with many names.

To find only one name for ourselves restricts us, because then we have only one way to respond to life, to others, to God. If my name is Responsible, I will respond to everything in an orderly, no-nonsense fashion. If my name is Joker, everything in life will be cause for laughter and turned into a joke. If my name is Victim, I will see the world as dangerous and out to get me. If my name is Teacher, I will always have a lesson for you. None of these responses is wrong, but each one lived out all the time limits us and keeps us locked into one way of being.

God's many names and our many names reveal the richness of who God is and who we are—multifaceted, complex, and mysterious. We are even more rich and varied than the names that others call us. For within our identity are many more parts that add to the fullness of who we are. Sometimes I am like a wise old woman; sometimes, like a mischievous young boy. I can think and feel and act from my competitive part, or my judgmental part, or my self-righteous part. Many situations bring out the mother in me, but when I am sick I behave like a young and fretful child. Within my identity I have both a cowardly lion and the goddess Artemis, protector of young women. Sometimes I am the rabbit of *Alice in Wonderland*, running frantically about, shouting, "I'm late! I'm late!" I am a dancer and a poet, a contemplative and a dreamer, a sadly wounded child.

As the names of God are infinite, so are our names infinite. Made in the image of God, we are many in one. Thinking of ourselves in this expanded

91

way is sometimes difficult, because it may contradict teachings of the past. As one man exclaimed to me: "I've spent the last forty years trying to discover who I am, who the real me is, getting myself together. Now you are suggesting there is no one answer to who I am? That I am shifting and changing all the time? I'm not sure I like this idea!"

And yet, as he explored the idea and himself, he realized that the model was true for him. He could recognize and name his many parts and he discovered a freedom he had not felt before. "I've been trying to be so grown up," he said, "responsible, caring, productive. I am all those things, but what a bore to be that *all* the time. I need to kick up my heels and play and take days off. I was too locked into whom I thought I was supposed to become before the age of fifty!"

Experiencing God through a variety of images and experiencing ourselves with many names gives us the opportunity to relate to God in an infinite number of ways. Our relationship with God becomes lively and spontaneous, open to explorations and new ways of being. The relationship also becomes deeper and more trusting as we become willing to reveal more and more of ourselves to God, knowing that God will be able to meet us in new and surprising ways.

One Person, Many Prayers

We may realize that we are made up of many parts, but wonder how to begin to recognize and name them. One way is simply to list the many ways you are in the world, the many roles you play, and the many qualities and values that guide your life. You may be a parent and a son or daughter. You may be an accountant or a bus driver or a homemaker or a teacher or a nurse. You may be responsible or fun-loving or solitary or extroverted. You may be all of these things and many more.

Another way to recognize our many parts is through the imagination. Imagine for a moment that you are in a theater, all by yourself, in a comfortable seat front row center. You are here not to see a play or a musical, but rather to see the many parts of who you are up on the stage. When you are ready, let the curtain go up and ask some of your many parts to present themselves to you. Let them appear one at a time, noticing their movement as they come on stage. What are they wearing? How do they hold their bodies? How do they name themselves? You will probably see some of your most familiar parts, but some new part might reveal itself.

When I first did this imagination activity, I saw my sportswoman dressed in hiking clothes, a small girl in a ruffled dress with patent leather

Mary Janes, and a teacher holding chalk and a ruler. These parts were very familiar, but then on stage strode a man in a three-piece business suit who was followed by a wizened old woman. Both of these parts surprised me. I had not thought of myself as old, but was encouraged to see that maybe I had a wise old woman within me. The man bothered me, because I did not think of myself as masculine, or particularly proper, but on further reflection I realized that he was the part of me who had a conservative outlook on life, who was cautious with money, and who liked everything in order.

Some of your parts may worry or frighten you. Others may delight you. Some of your parts may present themselves as animals or objects. See if you are willing to simply see and accept who (or what) appears without trying to figure them out, or judge them, or exclude them. Each part of ourselves offers a gift to the whole of who we are, even if we are not yet clear what the gift might be.

As you watch your many parts present themselves to you, you might choose one of your parts to get to know better and discover what that part can teach you about prayer. Ask it to step forward and tell you its name. Ask what it thinks about and how it feels. Ask what it wants and needs from you. Then ask how it experiences God and how it prays. Listen for the answers and see what you might learn about yourself and your options for prayer. When I asked my three-piece-suited businessman how he prayed, he said: "I don't pray with words. I work in my church." His answer delighted me, because I had always wondered if volunteer work were a form of prayer. This part of me certainly thought it was!

When you have learned what you can from the many parts of yourself, let the curtain come down on your stage. Reflect for a moment on what you have experienced. Remember that all may not be clear and comfortable, but with even one new insight, you are on your way to discovering how your many parts can teach you how to pray.

Each of our many parts has a preferred prayer style. The poet in me likes to craft beautiful phrases, making the words come together with precision. My dancer never speaks her prayers; she simply moves, knowing that every position, each rhythm is her prayer. The contemplative longs for quiet and stillness and the experience of resting in God beneath all words and images. The wounded child reaches for crayons and draws her prayers. As we are willing to name and get to know the many parts of ourselves, more and more prayer forms become available.

After doing this activity and reflecting for a while on what they had learned, a number of students described parts of themselves and how these parts taught them to pray:

"I have a part of myself I call Speedy. Speedy loves movement and play and always wears comfortable clothes, not caring how he looks. Speedy is learning to juggle, not because he particularly wants to succeed, but because it is great fun. Juggling is Speedy's prayer. He drops the balls and laughs and laughs, knowing God shares his delight."

"I have a very angry part of myself that comes in the form of a furry little gnome. He sputters and growls and stomps around a lot. When I mimed that part of myself and began to stomp around, I realized that stomping is his prayer."

A young woman recognized a part of herself as a rock. The rock was large and smooth and immobile. She thought at first that it was a paralyzed part of herself, but she came to know it as the very ground of her being. "This part prays by simply accepting God's love, just as a rock accepts the warmth from the sun. This is the part of me that prays without ceasing."

"I have a part of myself I call Snow Queen, who is not very forgiving. The Snow Queen spends hours designing fanciful ways to get even with the people who have wronged her. I told her she should be loving toward these people, forgiving them and turning the other cheek. But then the Snow Queen discovered the Psalms! "Oh God let them vanish like water that runs away; like grass let them be trodden down and wither. Let them be like the snail that dissolves into slime. . . . " (Ps. 58:7-8a) Oh, she loves those Psalms of vengeance! Now she prays and does not have to hold on to her resentment. She turns her fantasies of revenge over to God."

"I have a part of myself that is a coyote—watchful, still, powerful. I was not sure how this part of myself prayed until I thought about the coyote throughout the cycle of the day and the night. I imagined her howling at the moon. I realized her voice was her prayer. So now when I sing, alone or in the choir, I know that it is my coyote part at prayer."

Juggling, stomping, receiving God's love, praying the Psalms, singing— all are prayers. These people did not discover the one way to pray. They are not praying only with juggling balls, angry feet, stillness, vengeance, or song. They have simply found new ways to pray that come from a deep part of who they are. By opening up to the messages of hidden parts of themselves, these people are beginning to pray with all of who they are, holding nothing back from God. They are truly praying with body and soul.

Blocks to Prayer

Paul said about himself:

"I do not understand my own actions. For I do not do what I want, but I do the very thing I hate" (Romans 7:15).

These words could well apply to us when we long to pray and do not pray. Even with all the new ways to pray we may have discovered, we still do not pray as we want. We may forget to turn our attention to God in the midst of daily tasks. We may have bought the crayons but have not picked them up. We may have heard the Bible read in worship but did not allow our imagination to lead us into prayer. We may have walked through God's beautiful creation with our senses closed down. What is happening when we want to pray and we don't pray?

Understanding the many parts of ourselves can help us unravel this puzzle. Just as we have parts of ourselves that each have their own unique relationships to God, we may have parts of ourselves who feel disconnected from God, who doubt God's existence, or who may think that prayer is useless. We may have parts of ourselves who hold on to one narrow image of God, and that image does not inspire trust or invite intimacy. Parts of ourselves may question the efficacy of prayer, or may wonder if we are worthy to come into God's presence. These parts of ourselves may keep us from praying even as we long to respond to God through prayer.

Sometimes if we just think about what is going on in our lives, we can identify the blocks to prayer. But sometimes the dynamic is more subtle, more hidden, and not readily apparent. Then our imaginations can help us identify the parts of ourselves that are blocking our prayer life.

To help students or retreatants uncover these parts I invite them into a guided imagery designed to reveal the inner dynamic of "pray/don't pray." I invite them to settle into a comfortable position and take a moment to attend to their breathing. As they get comfortable, they allow their eyes to close. They take a moment to pay attention to their bodies, then to their feelings, and then to their minds, simply being aware of what is going on. I then ask them to imagine themselves in a favorite prayer place and to see themselves deep in prayer. I invite them to become the pray-er and feel the experience in their bodies and souls. I then suggest that something is suddenly going to interrupt them and pull them away from prayer.

After a long pause I invite them to look closely at their interruption to notice its size and shape, whether it is known or unknown. Some of the interruptions that have been reported are crying children, dogs scratching at the door, a loud bang, someone needing something, a list of things to do, a familiar person judging them. I suggest that they dialogue with the interruption to discover what the interruption wants and needs, what it thinks and feels. I invite the participants to listen and to respond with compassion, trying to discover everything there is to know about the interruption. I remind them that they can return to prayer whenever they wish — God will always be waiting — but right now their task is to attend lovingly to whatever interrupted them.

When the dialogue is complete, I suggest that they invite the interruption to join them in prayer and see what happens to them, to the interruption, and to the prayer. I give them all the time they need and then invite them to slowly return to the present moment, moving their bodies, gently opening their eyes. I encourage them to write and to draw their experience.

Many important things are often discovered in this activity. First, the interruption has been seen and named with compassion. Second, the interruption has been allowed to speak its truth and has been heard and accepted. Third, the interruption has been invited into and included in the life of prayer. This activity does not immediately resolve the "pray/don't pray" dilemma, but it does provide information and often points the way for healing and reconciliation to occur between two parts in conflict.

In one such activity, a man was interrupted by a weeping, dirty, wounded little boy. When the man turned his attention on the child, he imagined him saying: "You pretend that I don't exist. You are trying so hard to be successful, and now with your prayers you are trying to be holy. I am part of you. I need your love. Take me with you." Although the message was hard to hear, the man knew it held truth. In his imagination, he got off his knees and reached out to the little boy. Then, changing his prayer position, he held the child while he prayed.

Another participant was interrupted by a large figure dressed in active sportswear. This figure did not wait to be invited to speak; as soon as he got the attention of the woman in prayer, he told her to stop wasting her time with this foolishness. There was work to be done, money to be made, children to be fed. The woman reported that the voice was so strong that she almost stopped the imagery to obey this busy, responsible part of herself. But instead she invited him to pray with her. He refused. She then imagined herself saying gently, "It is your choice. But wait quietly until I am finished and then I will join you." She was amazed that he followed her wishes and interrupted her no more.

Many people get interrupted by figures in a variety of forms telling them that they are not praying right, that they shouldn't pray the way they are praying, or that they should pray some other way. Other common interruptions are doubts about whether God really cares or how God could possibly love us. Some interruptions believe God has more important things to do than listen to these personal prayers. The interruptions often come in human form, but people report also animals, objects, and sometimes just words or simply noise.

Some interruptions are eager to join in prayer, others are more reluctant, and some absolutely refuse. One student was interrupted by a part of himself who was an atheist. This part ridiculed him for even believing in prayer, let alone actively praying. This discovery was disturbing because he was in seminary preparing for the ministry. But when he recognized this part he was able to step back from the raging battle within and see that the believer was stronger than the atheist. He also realized that he would meet nonbelievers in his ministry, and he needed to learn to treat them with compassion. He could begin by having compassion for the atheist within.

One response to the invitation to pray is not better than another. A part joining in prayer does not indicate more spiritual maturity than a part that resists. The interruption's reaction to the invitation simply gives information to the pray-er about the nature of the block to prayer. Those parts that hesitate or refuse to pray may need to be reassured that they will not be ignored, but also that they will not be allowed to interrupt prayer time. Sometimes an agreement can be made regarding time and energy. "I will take thirty minutes for my prayer in the morning and then I will get to work."

I believe that all parts of us, the ones who teach us to pray and the ones who block us from prayer, bring a gift to the wholeness of who we are. Our hardworking parts, the parts that want us to get it "right," the parts that need reassurance of our worth and the unconditional love of God—all make up the richness of who we are. A man whose prayer was interrupted by a cynical doubter declared, "With that part around I surely am not in danger of joining a cult. That part would keep me asking the hard questions."

Many of us were taught that to be acceptable to God, to be truly faithful, to become good Christians we had to overcome our doubt, learn never to judge, forgive immediately, and get rid of our anger and our jealousies. Somehow we were to peel away all that was "bad" and remain eternally "good." I call this "stripped-down holiness." This form of holiness leaves us brittle and dry, leads often to self-righteousness and pride. Stripped-down holiness denies body and soul.

When we recognize all of our parts as gifts to be honored and added to the self we bring before God in prayer, we have a rich and pregnant holiness. Some of our parts may be stuck and in need of transformation; some of our parts may be wounded and in need of healing; some of our parts may be capable of sin. All that is true. But no part of us is to be shunned, ignored, or cast off. Jesus calls us all to the table, particularly those in need of transformation, healing, and forgiveness. Imagine all your many parts gathered at the table of the Lord. Imagine the conversations, the arguments, the laughter and the tears. Imagine that the door is open. No one is excluded and no one is sent away. All are welcomed. All are loved. This is an image of wholeness. This is humankind made in the image of God.

Bible Stories Within

In prayer class the week before Palm Sunday, I laid cards on the floor with the names of the participants of Holy Week face down—a scribe, Judas, Pilate, Mary Magdalene, the woman at Bethany, Peter, a soldier, Mary the mother of Jesus, Simon of Cyrene, Barabbas. Each student was asked to pick one card sight unseen, find the biblical references to that person in the Easter story, then approach all of the Holy Week events through the eyes of that character. What did he see? What did she feel? How did he react and respond? How did the Easter event affect the rest of her life? What new ways to pray were opened up when they recognized the people of the Bible representing parts of who they are?

The students reported that during Holy Week they discovered a new depth to a familiar story. They used their imaginations to explore how their person might have been before or after they are mentioned in the story. One student identified with Mary, watching her son put through trial, agony, humiliation, and death. Another took the role of Simon of Cyrene, identifying what it would have been like to be called from the crowd to carry the cross of Jesus. Imagining the life of Barabbas after he had been set free, another student found in himself a part that needed liberation.

One woman who had selected Peter found this exercise not only illuminating about the Easter story, but also very revealing about herself. "I became Peter for that week," she said, "going where he went, saying what he said, feeling what he felt. Not only did I get a new view of Holy Week. I discovered something about myself—I am Peter. Or, more accurately, I have a Peter within."

Finding the part of herself who was like Peter was distressing at first but ultimately healing. When she read the account of Peter's betrayal of Jesus (Mark 14:66-72), she remembered a time when she had betrayed a friend. She remembered how she had thought she would never turn away from a friend in need, how she had judged other people who had. She remembered the incident of betrayal, and the terrible feelings afterward. She had done nothing to repair the broken relationship and she still felt guilty and ashamed although the betrayal had occurred many years before. She felt stuck in her guilt, because her friend had died, and she could not go to her for forgiveness. She had prayed about the incident and felt God had forgiven her, but she could not forgive herself.

Recognizing her own act of betrayal, she identified with Peter in the moment he realizes what he has done. Then the words leapt out of her as if she had never seen them before: "And he broke down and wept." She realized she had never wept those tears of anguish over denying a friend. She had cried at her death, but not about the act of betrayal. Freed by the biblical words and the picture of Peter weeping, she began to cry. The tears coursed down her face. She was wracked with sobs, crying at last for herself, her betrayal, the lost friendship, and her friend.

"The tears have set me free," she said. "I have spent so much time in regret, chastising myself, reminding myself what a terrible thing I had done, I had not realized I was carrying around a wound that needed healing. My tears were the beginning of the healing process. My tears were a new and different form of prayer."

She was also comforted that the story of Peter does not end with his weeping. Peter goes on in his life, recognizing Jesus after the resurrection, spreading the good news. She realized that her call was to move on in her life, striving to honor her present and future friends with love and honesty and realistic commitment.

When I was in seminary, I took part in a similar activity using the images of the people of the Easter story. We students were invited to write a meditation from the perspective of the character we chose. I selected the woman at Bethany (Mark 14:3-9) and tried to imagine how she had first met Jesus and what had led her to perform her loving, extravagant act of anointing Jesus. In so doing, I realized that this unnamed woman was a part of myself.

He Never Knew My Name

He never knew my name, but he knew my heart. He never knew my name, but he accepted my gift. The others saw only a woman stepping over her bounds, breaking the limits of tradition, walking where she was unwelcome, assuming a role that men held sacred. The others did not see me, but the man called Jesus knew my love. He never knew my name, but he knew my heart.

A week ago, I would never have believed that I could have done such a spontaneous, impulsive, extravagant thing. For I am a very practical woman: steadfast, hardworking, and strong, but docile and obedient to the words of the men and the ways of my tradition. Rarely do I speak out. I know my place. I care for my household, my children, my husband, and my husband's parents. I tend, I scold, I love, I plan, I scheme. I meet everyone's needs. I am righteous in the fulfilling of my duties.

But last week, I was caught so unaware. It all came as such a surprise! I had gone out to market. I had my bags and bundles. I was shopping and trading and gossiping as I usually do. I then became aware of the clamor of hurrying crowds. I felt the ground move with the running of feet. Excitement was in the air, and I was simply on my way to market!

But the moment caught hold of me. I found myself rushing with the others toward the center of the city. The crowds were deep, undulating and noisy. I heard the words: "Hosanna! Hosanna! Make way for the one who comes in the name of the *Lord*!"

I had to push, rudely using my elbows, trying to catch a glimpse of the one the crowds were welcoming. I broke through to the front. I could hardly believe my eyes. What I saw was a simple, tired man riding on a donkey.

"Is that all?" I scoffed to myself. "A tired young man on a donkey?"

And then, as I stood there watching, he turned and looked directly at me. His deep, dark eyes looked through my scoffing, through my rudeness, through my righteousness, and through my busy self-importance. He looked into my eyes and he saw me. He did not know my name, but he saw my heart.

The next few days, my heart would not be still. I raced about trying to learn all I could about the man I had seen, the man people called Jesus. I listened about the house and in the marketplace, even moving close to strangers to hear what they had to say. I grew bold and asked questions of the menfolk of my household. They answered me with disdain, telling me to leave the business of the temple to the men. But I kept listening, and I kept learning.

One day I went to hear him speak. He told a story, something about a vineyard. I did not understand all his words. He seemed to speak in riddles. But my heart responded to his voice. He did not know I was in that crowd, but he spoke directly to me. My heart quickened in response.

Later that day, I learned that Jesus was upsetting the authorities. They did not know what to do with him. The whole city was in confusion, a veritable uproar. In my household as well. But as the confusion mounted around me, the chaos of my heart quieted, and I began to experience a peace and strength far beyond my imaginings. Somehow the man called Jesus had entered my heart. I had no idea what this meant: "entered my heart." But the experience was real.

Two days before Passover and the feast of Unleavened Bread, I learned that Jesus was to dine at the home of Simon, the man healed of his skin disease by one of Jesus' miraculous acts. We all still called him Simon the Leper, and he lived on my street. Jesus was soon to dine *on my street*!

I knew I had to go to him. Of course I was not invited! But I had to go. I wanted once, just once, to get close to this man called Jesus. He did not know my name, but I knew he was waiting for me.

As I left my house that evening, I caught sight of the alabaster jar that contains pure, liquid nard, a fragrant oil, our household treasure! With no further thought, I reached out for the jar. Clutching it tightly against my breast, I moved silently out onto the street on my way to the man called Jesus.

I must stop at this point to remind you that I had always been a practical woman, careful, prudent, frugal. I watched the household money like a hawk. I was generous in my manner, but never given to careless spending. My taking of the jar of nard was greatly out of character. Even going out at night alone was not my usual pattern. All the acts of that night were disobedient to my traditional roles. But for the first time in my life I was obeying the call of my heart.

I arrived at the house of Simon the Leper, a small, poor house, but festive with the sounds of a friendly gathering. As I stood in the doorway, I could hear the murmur of voices, the movement of feet, and the rustle of people settling down for a meal. I could smell the food, the warm bodies crowded into that small space, and the perfume of flowers in the air of the courtyard.

As I moved just inside the doorway I could see the men reclining at the table, smiling, nodding to one another and beginning to eat from a large common bowl. Jesus was at the center of the group, and as I stood watching from the shadows, he looked up from his companions, directly into my eyes. He did not know my name, but silently he called me to him.

No words were spoken between us. The other men did not know I was there. They only noticed me when I took my place directly behind Jesus. With sure, fast motions, I broke the alabaster jar, pouring the entire store of liquid nard over his head. Fragrance filled the room, and all watched in amazement as I rubbed the oil into his forehead, his scalp, and down around his neck where it had dripped.

In the silence, time stood still. I heard ringing in my heart, the Holy Word of God telling of Samuel anointing Saul to be prince over the people of Israel:

> And you shall reign over the people
> of the Lord and you will save them from
> the hand of their enemies.

But just as surely as I knew those words, I knew I was anointing Jesus for another purpose. I knew that this anointment was for burial, not for coronation. I knew this not from Scripture but from the wisdom of birth and death that rests in the depth of women. Knowing the future, I rubbed the fragrant oil even more tenderly into the head of this man who was soon to die.

My ministry was abruptly broken by the voices of the indignant men:

> "Who invited that woman in here?"
> "No woman should be touching Jesus like that."
> "What a terrible, wasteful thing to do!"
> "She should give the money to the poor."
> "Throw her out!"

They were angry with me, calling me foolish, condemning my extravagance. They could see only the broken jar, the broken traditions, the broken pleasure of their dinner party. They could not see that which remained unbroken: love.

But Jesus saw. He did not know my name, but he knew my heart. He knew that my pouring forth of the oil was an extravagant act of love.

As I turned to leave, I heard Jesus' voice above all the others saying:

> Leave her alone! She has done a beautiful thing to me. She did what she could. She has anointed my body for burying. You will always have the poor with you, but you will not always have me. Wherever the gospel is preached in the whole world, what she has done will be told in memory of her.

I walked slowly and silently home, at peace within myself. Jesus will never know my name, but he knows my heart. His final words, "in memory of her," fill my being at this moment. And I know now that all my deeds will be done in memory of him. All my deeds—in fact, my very life—in memory of him.

In writing this meditation, I identified with the curious scoffing part of myself as well as the part that was willing to take risks and act in defiance of established norms. I also identified with the power and process of conversion and caught a glimpse of how this conversion could change my life forever. Since writing this meditation I can no longer simply observe Holy Week. I have become an active participant in the last week of Jesus' life.

You do not need to expand a story to this extent to find yourselves in many of the stories of the Bible. Maybe you have a part who is like Moses, doubting your ability to obey God's call: "Oh my Lord, I have never been eloquent, neither in the past nor even now that you have spoken to your servant; but I am slow of speech and slow of tongue" (Exod. 4:10). Maybe you have a part that is like Ruth, willing to make a total commitment: "Where you go, I will go; where you lodge, I will lodge; your people shall be my people, and your God my God (Ruth 1:16). Maybe there is a part of you seeking power and position like James and John. "And they said to Jesus, 'Grant us to sit, one at your right hand and one at your left, in your glory'" (Mark 10:37).

The Bible reveals to us the glory of God at work in human history. It also reveals to us the workings of our own souls. When we are willing to recognize parts of ourselves in the stories, we become an integral part of the story. I am the hypocrite who stands on the street corner praying so others will notice (Matt. 6:5). I am the woman with enough faith to reach out to simply touch the hem of Jesus' garment, knowing I will be healed (Luke 8:44). I am Pilate, who washes my hands of responsibility and allows others to make the hard choices for me (Mark 15:6-15). I am Mary, who wants to sit at the feet of Jesus, and I am Martha, busy and worried about my many tasks (Luke 10:38-42). I am the prodigal son, who has squandered my birthright, and I am the elder son, responsible, angry, and self-righteous (Luke 15:11-42).

"There is within you a lion and a lamb," wrote Henri Nouwen. "Spiritual maturity is the ability to let lamb and lion lie down together."[1] The lion is the image of the part of yourself that is strong and resourceful and responsible. The lion makes choices, acts quickly, and is wise in the ways of the world. The lamb is the vulnerable part of yourself that is afraid, dependent, in need of love and support. The lamb knows what it is like to cling to God. To live in only the lion or the lamb denies the important gift of the other. When you honor both "you can act assertively without denying your own needs. And you can ask for affection and care without betraying your talent to offer leadership. . . . The kingdom of peace that Jesus came to establish begins when your lion and your lamb can freely and fearlessly lie down together."[2]

If we are all these parts (lion, lamb, Mary, Martha, Pilate, Peter, dancer, child, and many more), how will we sort ourselves out? Sorting, arranging, controlling, fixing, and analyzing are not our tasks. Bringing to consciousness all of who we are is what we are to do. We are to open ourselves to all of who we are and then bring that consciousness, that understanding, and that confusion to God in prayer. John Sanford names the claiming of our overlooked and unclaimed parts of ourselves as the work of the soul. "For as long as we are seeking consciousness we keep our soul, but if we renounce consciousness and reject what belongs to us, banishing it into darkness, we lose our soul. With the connection with the soul, the whole of ourselves may begin to come into conscious expression."[3]

Is that not what God wants for all God's people? To bring all of who we are into the world, into relationships, into service, into play, into prayer? Understanding the fullness, the richness, and the complexity of who we are brings a whole new meaning to the little boy's prayer that I cited in chapter 2: "Hello God! Here I am!"

ACTIVITIES FOR REFLECTION AND DISCUSSION

1. At the top of a piece of paper, write the question, "Who am I?" Begin to write down the many ways you name yourself. Identify yourself by the roles you play, by your interests, by your feelings. Imagine characters in stories or in the Bible, identify with animals, flowers, or other objects. Start the list and then add to it during the next few days, keeping alive the intriguing question, "Who am I?" You may be surprised how many ways you can name yourself.

2. Sit with your list and pick out parts of yourself you believe are essential to who you are. As you choose, ask yourself slowly, gently, "How does this part of me pray?" Maybe you will not know, maybe it will remain a puzzle. If no answer comes, go to another part and ask yourself, "How does this part pray?" See if you are willing to accept as answers *anything* that deepens your relationship to God.

3. Do the guided imagery on pages 95–96 by yourself or with a friend. After you have discovered an interruption and dialogued with it and invited it to pray with you, write or draw a response to the discovery. Keep your heart open to the interruption, accepting it with compassion, honoring its gift to you. If the interruption has its own way to pray, explore praying in that manner. If the interruption showed any signs of willingness to pray with you, intentionally invite it into your next prayer time. Play with the dynamics you have discovered. Try not to work too hard!

4. Have you ever identified with a person in a Bible story? When you read the story of Moses resisting God's call (Exod. 4:10-17), does it feel familiar? When you read of Miriam leading other women in song and dance in gratitude for God's victory (Exod. 15:20-21), do you feel a stirring of your own soul? In the Christmas story do you identify with Mary or Joseph, or with the shepherds who were so afraid, or the wise men who traveled far distances to pay homage to the baby Jesus? Do you ever feel like the innkeeper who turned the struggling couple away?

When you read or hear Bible stories, play with the idea that some person in the story could reflect a part of who you are. Be aware that it is more pleasurable to identify with the good Samaritan than it is to identify with Judas, but each identification might point you to a more complete understanding of who you are. Each identification may also reveal new ways to be in prayer.

7

ACTION PRAYERS:
WORK, SERVICE, JUSTICE,
AND CARE OF THE EARTH

Years ago I saw a sign over the desk of a secretary: "Work is love made visible." I was startled, because I could understand the phrase in relation to some work such as caring for children, or planting a garden, or writing a book, or serving on the board of a nonprofit organization, but I had difficulty with the idea that the routine work of an office could in fact be motivated by love. And yet, as I got to know the woman whose desk it was, I realized she did live according to her motto. These words were not empty words. She experienced all of her tasks, even the most menial, as loving service. She had a stillness about her even at her busiest moments. This woman lived a balance of contemplation and action. In times of stress, when others around her were agitated and distraught, she was able to continue her work smoothly and purposefully, and in so doing calmed the entire office.

Contemplation and Action

The tensions between prayer and work, or contemplation and action, have been the topic of much discussion and argument. Some people put all their energy into prayer, believing that through prayer God will act in the world. Other people put all their energy into work, believing that only through the efforts of human hands and hearts will the work of the world get done. Still others see the need for both prayer and work but are puzzled whether one is more important than the other. I believe that the tensions we experience are actually not between *contemplation* and *action,* but between *contemplation* and *agitation* or between *action* and *escapism.*

Agitation is action without soul, action for the sake of action, action with conflicting purposes or without connection to meaning. The most vivid image and experience of agitation that I know is a group of teenagers trying to decide what to do on a Saturday night. Phones are ringing, options are tossed about, someone needs to leave, another wants some food, another searches the movie schedule. Just as it seems they are reaching a decision, the doorbell rings and two more youngsters arrive with new ideas. Now there are too many people for the cars they have, and the planning begins again. Finally some decision is made, and they troop out calling their good-byes, only to have someone turn back because he forgot his shoes, or she lost her keys. Out they go again. The house falls silent for a moment, then they all return because they have discovered they don't have enough money for the proposed activity. The process of decision begins once again. The agitation continues.

Escapism focuses only on the transcendent, eyes turned heavenward, mind attending to abstractions, heart longing for inner peace. Escapists "want to spend their hours lounging or drifting or gazing or 'processing.' They work only to sustain themselves and even then as little as possible. [Escapists] say they are seeking God in mystery, but as a matter of fact they are actually missing the presence of God in the things that give meaning to life."[1] In California in the 1970s, these people were called "awareness-junkies," those who were after more and more awareness but never able put their insights to work in their own lives or the lives of others.

In contrast to these polarized images are the blended images of active contemplatives and of prayerful purposeful workers. I have a clergy friend who has spent much of her adult life studying and practicing different forms of meditation and contemplative prayer. She practices daily and goes on regular retreats, some of them for extended periods of time. She also is married, has raised three children, has been a full-time pastor, and now serves in a hospital as a chaplain. I think of her as an example of an active contemplative.

Contemplative action can be found at many construction sites where men and women are at work. Everyone is busy. Many activities are happening at once. Some work alone, others in pairs, and at times all join on one task that needs the strength and talents of the group. A rhythm of silence and sound, talk and music rise and fall around the site. I wonder how everyone knows what to do and how it will all come together. But it does, because these workers share a plan and a vision. Even as they do the small tasks, they know what they are building. I know nothing of the prayer life of the workers, but I experience their work as contemplative. They are not agitated, but purposely active, involved in important work of the world.

The Rule of Saint Benedict refers to prayer and work in the same breath: "Idleness is the enemy of the soul. Therefore, the monastic should have specified periods for manual labor as well as for prayerful reading."[2] All members of the community are expected to work, no matter their age or ability. Good work can always be found that is appropriate to the individual, and that work "is not a nuisance to be avoided, [but] a gift to be given."[3] There need be no argument between contemplation and action, between prayer and work, because God calls us to both. God is calling us to prayer, calling us to action, calling us to love and serve the world. Work is a prayer of body and soul. "We work because the world is unfinished and it is ours to develop. We work with a vision in mind. . . . Work is a commitment to God's service."[4]

Service

The work we do in the world may in some way serves others. Teachers not only earn their living in the classroom, they also serve the children of the community. Farmers' work feeds millions. Government workers of all levels serve the nation by keeping democracy in motion. Maintenance crews serve us all by keeping buildings clean and safe. No matter what the work, others besides ourselves are served by the work of our hands, the work of our minds, the work we do to earn a living. But, in addition to this work, we are called to serve others directly.

In the last chapter of the Gospel of John (21:15-19), the risen Christ asks Peter three times whether Peter loves him. Each time, Peter responds, "Yes, Lord, you know that I love you." Each time, Jesus tells him, "Feed my sheep." To tend to Jesus' flock is a direct consequence of Peter's love for Jesus. Although Jesus was talking to Peter, his words were intended for all his disciples and for all his followers throughout the ages. We are called to love. We are called to serve those in need. Serving others is a call from God.

For service to be a prayer, our actions need to come from our relationship with God. In the words of Parker J. Palmer, author of *The Active Life*, our relationship with God "draws us deeper into right action by getting us more deeply in touch with the gifts that we have to give, with our need to give them, with the people and problems that need us."[5] If our service is not grounded in our relationship with God, we may serve from guilt or obligation, we may serve with hard hearts or with condescension or out of pity. Or, we may serve indiscriminately, giving reactively to whatever need presents itself.

There is so much need in the world today that we must practice discernment. We cannot meet every need that confronts us, and if we try, we find ourselves in a state of agitation rather than loving action. Or we may be tempted to believe that there is nothing we can do in the face of such need and escape into our own worlds, closing our hearts to those outside our immediate family and friends.

A young man at college was faced with such a dilemma. Posters were everywhere asking for help for specific groups of people. Invitations were constant to march for one cause or another. The interfaith group he attended offered many opportunities to serve in the college community and in the life of the city beyond. Early in his first year, he tried to respond to all the interesting requests for his time and energy. He began to feel scattered, unable to focus on any service project, let alone his studies. Then he decided to respond to nothing, reminding himself that he was at college to study and learn through the classes for which his parents were spending hard-earned money. He would wait until graduation to volunteer. But that choice did not feel right either, because he knew he had gifts that were needed now. And what were those gifts? A gift for language, an ability to relate to others, and a love of other cultures. He decided to get involved with a tutoring program that focused on teaching English to young immigrant children in the city schools. His tutoring became as integral to his college life as his classes and his friends, as each week he caught the bus to his assigned school. He knew he had made a wise choice and he continued with the commitment to "his kids" for four years.

Discernment is also needed in deciding how long we stay in a particular situation of loving service. A story is told of the Buddha who was called into service in a community of monks and nuns who were fighting among themselves.[6] Some were accusing others of not following the rules of the monastery. Those accused were accusing their accusers of judgment and self-righteousness. Meditation practice was disturbed, peaceful living was absent, and compassion for one another was nonexistent.

When the Buddha arrived, he spoke with the monks and nuns, encouraging them to ask each other for forgiveness and to forgive readily from their hearts. The monastics took that advice into their disagreements and began to argue about what had been done that was wrong so that forgiveness could be requested and given. Conflict erupted in response to every suggestion the Buddha offered, so after a few days the Buddha left, leaving the monks and nuns to their own devices. The Buddha then took a short vacation in the forest, where all was peaceful and calm, knowing he had done what he could.[6]

Service becomes a prayer when we serve our sisters and brothers with love and compassion that comes from God. If we forget that God is the source of our love, we deplete ourselves and end up serving from our emptiness rather than our fullness. People in the helping professions often speak about becoming drained, feeling dry, wondering if they have anything left to give. I believe these experiences occur not only when we forget to turn to God to be filled with love, but also when we forget to treat ourselves with the same love and compassion with which we treat our neighbors.

Treating ourselves with compassion is recognizing that our gifts, our time, and our energy are limited. We cannot be all things to all people. When we begin to think otherwise, we run the risk not only of depletion and exhaustion but also of arrogance. Only God is everything to everyone.

Practicing compassion toward ourselves is not "self-serving." Rather, having compassion for ourselves is including ourselves among the needy we are called to serve. Both the college student and the Buddha showed compassion toward themselves even as they went forth to serve others. The young man recognized his time and energy were limited and had the courage to say "no" to many things so he could say "yes" to the one thing he could do with all his heart. The Buddha responded to a call for help, but when he realized that his presence and his gifts were not of use to these people, he had the courage to leave with the task undone.

Showing compassion for ourselves does not get in the way of our prayers of service. Showing compassion for ourselves allows us to serve from a full and grateful heart. Jesus showed compassion for himself when he went off by himself to pray. He knew he could not continue his ministry without being filled with the love and power of God. A minister showed compassion for herself when she took her two-week vacation with her family, even though members of her congregation were unhappy that she would not officiate at the wedding of the daughter of a longtime member. A retired office manager showed compassion for himself when he turned down an invitation to serve on a board which regularly met at night. "I no longer go out in the evening," he said. "My wife likes me home, and besides, evening meetings make the next day very unproductive." The mother of young children showed compassion for herself when she told her church she would not teach first-grade Sunday school. "I do not need more time with children," she told the caller. "I would be happy to serve the church in some way that puts me in contact with adults!"

To serve with love and compassion, for prayer and service to become one, we might attend to the order of love in the great commandment: "You shall love the Lord your God with all your heart, and with all your soul, and all your strength, and with all your mind and your neighbor as yourself."

Peace and Justice

"If you want peace, work for justice" a familiar bumper sticker proclaims. When we work and serve with a biblical vision to guide us, I believe that vision is some form of a just and peaceful world. Throughout the Bible, the call for justice is as strong as the call for love. Jonah was sent by God to Nineveh to tell the people that their behavior was not in accord with God's love of justice and peace. Isaiah gave us the image of the wolf living peacefully with the lamb. The psalmist cried out for justice when he was surrounded by enemies who had wronged him. The prophet Micah said: "And what does the Lord require of you but to do justice, and to love kindness and to walk humbly with your God?" (Micah 6:8).

In the Christian scriptures, John the Baptist cried out against injustice, preparing the way for Jesus and his teachings. Jesus taught about justice for the marginalized—the widows, the orphans, the ill, and the old. Jesus called his listeners to responsibility for the religious laws that did not serve all the people but placed some above others with privilege and power. Jesus wanted to turn the unjust world of his time upside down so that the first would be last, and the last would be first, and all would be welcome at the table of the Lord.

Jesus is often seen as a peacemaker. He invited the little children to come to him. He mediated disputes among his disciples. He preached compassion and forgiveness. But Jesus also said that he came not to bring peace but the sword. This statement is confusing. How does the image of a sword relate to the call for peace and justice in the world?

I believe this passage in the Bible invites us to look at the complexity of peace and justice and the difficulty of working toward a just and peaceful world. When Jesus called the religious leaders of his day to repent the wrong they were doing to others, he raised a sword to the establishment. His sword was not a sword of violence; it was the sword of truth. Jesus' sword called others to awareness and into radical action. Jesus' words and actions were not experienced as peaceful, but were seen by religious and secular leaders as a threat to the peace they were enjoying at the expense of other people.

Acts of justice are not easy; working for peace does not come without sacrifice. To find peace in a warring world, to create justice when injustice rules is to engage in conflict, or even to create conflict where none is seen to exist.

In the United States, women were not allowed to vote until 1928. Before that time the male privilege of voting went unquestioned. To bring about justice, some had to say: "This is not right!" When people began to speak out, conflicts arose, sides were drawn, and those who spoke were accused of disrupting the peace. The experience was the same for the Abolitionists fighting against slavery and for the civil rights activists of the 1950s and 1960s fighting against segregation. All these individuals and groups brought their call for justice to a world that was living under what was declared by those in power to be "the natural order of things," a world that had no desire to change. The people who spoke out and rallied and wrote letters and pamphlets and marched for justice did not bring peace; they brought the sword.

The desire for everything to be peaceful may serve to perpetuate injustice. True peace follows the establishment of justice. Justice comes when an unjust pattern or system is ended. But everyone does not welcome the termination of the way things are. People fight against change. In many cases, they believe that *they* are the ones fighting for justice, while those attempting to bring in a new order are self-serving and unjust in their beliefs and accusations and actions.

An institution in which I taught was engaged in a struggle for justice. Two issues were brought to the fore as rallying points. First, an organization of students of color accused the administration of tolerating and even promoting institutional racism. Second, a woman faculty member was denied tenure, and many students and faculty questioned the process used to reach that decision. A number accused the administration of misuse of power. Faculty, students, and staff wrote letters and held meetings. People joined together in prayer. Angry confrontations occurred. In pursuit of their demands, eight students began a fast, which they broke only with water and daily communion.

Even with all this activity, nothing immediately changed, but the equilibrium of the community was deeply disturbed. Faculty and students took class time from their planned lessons to discuss the issues. Worship leaders designed chapel services to ease the pain that so many people were feeling. Finally, concessions were made on both sides. The students ended their fast, and a mediation team was hired to help the community work through the grievances. A process of change and restructuring was put into place; reconciliation and healing began.

In this quiet aftermath, a student came to my office, sat down quietly, and asked, "Do you believe that prayer and spirituality are connected to the struggle for justice? Does prayer lead you into action or help you avoid action? Were you involved? Where did you stand?" Her intense but gentle and respectful questions pushed me to articulate the conflict that had been going on in me since the struggle had begun and to talk about the actions I had taken for peace and justice. I welcomed the opportunity to express the self-questioning and decision making that had been occurring in my heart since the beginning of the struggle.

I had prayed for all involved: the institution, the protesting students and their supporters, other students who were confused and disillusioned, staff who were often caught in the middle of the struggle, and all the faculty and administrators who were divided among themselves. Prayer felt important and necessary. Prayer was easy. I wondered whether there was something else I was called to do, some action I needed to take in addition to prayer.

I knew myself well enough to recognize the part of me that wanted to run away at the first sign of conflict. This part believed she has no voice and no power, that her presence would be of no use, and that if she became involved, something terrible would happen. I also had a part that wanted to get involved instantly, choose my side, and fight to the finish. But neither of these parts of myself seemed to fit the struggle for justice that was before me. Because I believe and try to live out the idea that true prayer pulls us more fully into the world, I could not run away and only pray. Because I have been the victim of institutional oppression and because I have also administered to the best of my ability and still been accused of unfairness and privilege, I could not stand with either side against the other. I wondered whether there was anything left for me to do.

I decided not to go to the many meetings at which the history of the issues was laid out, where feelings were aired, where accusations were made and heard. I made this decision because I believed that attending the gatherings was not the best use of my limited time and energy. I decided what I could do was to stand as a pastoral presence to the students who were facing the same questions I was struggling with, and to stand as a liturgical presence to any group that requested my prayers and sacramental leadership. Therefore, within three weeks I took four actions. I served communion to the fasting students and their supporters. I led a mini-retreat for the staff on spiritual nurture in the midst of chaos. I participated in liturgical dance during a chapel service designed to present the struggle and offer a vision and a hope of reconciliation. At the invitation of the president, I wrote and offered the benediction at the graduation service.

In this deeply divisive struggle, did I act for justice? I know that some people believed I let them down by not taking a definite stand for their position. I know others felt that I was serving my own interests by responding to the invitations of all the people on both sides of the conflict who requested my presence. The student who initially asked me the question told me after our discussion that she now understood my reasons for taking the actions I did, and that although she respected them she did not agree with them.

I share this story of a struggle for justice to illuminate the complexities of the simple statement: "If you want peace, work for justice." If we are aware of the conflicts and complications inherent in the call to justice we will be prepared when suddenly we are called out from the peace of the way things are to contribute to the creation of a new order. What will we do? What will we say? How shall we pray? Rarely will we find one "just" position and one "unjust" position. We will need to search our hearts to discern what action we will take. And as we act and speak and pray, we would be wise to remember that the prophet Micah knew that doing justice went hand in hand with kindness and humility. As we respond to the call to justice, and as our prayers are turned into action, may our choices always reflect this ancient truth.

Stewardship of the Earth

The work of peace and justice goes beyond human relationships and institutions to include all of God's creatures and all of the earth. In Genesis 2:15 we are told to "till and keep" the garden, our earthly home. For those of us who live in cities, in homes and apartments far from the natural world, the only garden we may have to tend is a small patch of lawn, a small vegetable plot, or a few house plants. But as human beings, we are responsible for the care and safekeeping of the whole natural world. We are responsible not because the earth belongs to us, but because, in the words of Chief Seattle, "We belong to the earth."

Sometimes, we experience that belonging very directly. I have just returned from a two-hour walk in the springtime Rockies. The sky is brilliant blue, with puffy white clouds floating by. The open lands are turning green, and bright yellow dandelions blanket the hillsides. Streams are full to overflowing with runoff from the heavy winter snow. Some snow is still on the high peaks and lower shady areas, dotting the landscape with patches of white. Most of the aspen groves are in full leaf, while a few remain in the dormancy of winter. Scattered bulbs are pushing up through dry earth. A red fox runs across my path, and chipmunks are everywhere.

Now, outside this cabin where I write, the air is alive with hummingbirds. Cows and their calves graze contentedly. A black cat stretches in the evening sun. Old dog Jefferson woofs halfheartedly at a sound in the valley. I hear thunder in the distance. A storm is on the way. All day, all around me are the sights and sounds and smells of creation. How can anyone doubt a divine hand in this glorious beauty? The presence of God is everywhere.

Marcus Borg, professor of culture and religion, names this experience of God everywhere, God "right here," God surrounding all, God within all, panentheism. Panentheism is not to be confused with pantheism, which identifies the universe and all within it with God. Panentheism does not equate everything with God. Panentheism rather places God in everything and everything in God. "God is not to be identified with the sum total of things, rather, God is more than everything, even as God is present everywhere. God is all around us and within us, and we are within God."[7]

At first glance, this theology may seem confusing, particularly if we are used to imagining God "out there," somewhere beyond here. But remember the many ways we addressed God in prayer in chapter 5. Those names explored the mystery of who God is and the infinite ways God can be named. Panentheism explores the mystery of *where* God is, and identifies the infinite number of places God can be found. As an ancient Irish prayer proclaims:

God with me, God before me, God behind me,
God in me, God beneath me, God above me
God on my right, God on my left,
God when I lie down, God when I sit down,
    God when I arise,
God in the heart of everyone who thinks of me,
God in the mouth of everyone who speaks of me,
God in every eye that sees me,
God in every ear that hears me.[8]

Theologian Sallie McFague encourages us to think about where God is by naming the world as our meeting place with God.[9] The way we meet God in the world is through our relationship and interdependence with all other creatures on our planet. Therefore, our spirituality is not simply defined by our relationship to God but by our relationship with all of creation. Her theological model suggests that "God is closer to us than we are to ourselves, because God is the breath or spirit that gives life to the billions of different bodies that make up God's body. But God is also the source, power, and goal of everything that is, for the creation depends utterly upon God."[10]

The earth as the body of God may sound strange to us if we have always considered God to be spirit rather than matter. But just as God became present in Jesus in human form, could not God become present in all creation? "The Word was made flesh." "Glorify God in your bodies." Just as these phrases call us to rethink the ways we have divided body and soul, so do these theologies help us rethink the ways we have removed God from creation, the ways we have separated spirit and matter. As we imagine and experience God's presence everywhere, we are called to care more deeply and act more reverently toward the earth and all its creatures. Stewardship of the earth can become a prayer of body and soul.

Dancing for Universal Peace

While a number of people work and serve, tend the earth and all its creatures, and struggle for justice, many others are dancing for peace. "We believe that if people of different faiths and beliefs celebrate together the dances of their different traditions, they will discover a commonality and connection and have no need to fight," a young woman told me. I was in a large fellowship hall of a downtown Denver church for my first experience of dancing for universal peace.[11]

I arrived early, but many people had already gathered. In the center of the hall was a round rug, on which rested two guitars, a small drum, a flute, and a candle. People were sitting quietly, or talking in small groups. A man arrived with a little boy of about five. A group of women came in with a very excited young girl. A number of people sported gray hair. One woman proudly told me she was 78 and came to dance for peace almost every week. Although the group was predominately white, there were a number of people of other races and ethnic origins present. The participants were lively and friendly, and when Reverend Timothy Dobson, who leads this dance community, picked up his guitar and began to sing softly, everyone moved into a large circle, holding the hands of their neighbors.

Timothy welcomed us and gave a brief explanation of the invocation, which was drawn from the Islamic tradition. We then recited it three times in English. With each recitation, we took a step forward toward the lighted candle, symbolizing our quest for peace by moving as a community toward the center. After the opening, we formed three concentric circles, because by that time the participants numbered more than 120.

Our first dance was from the Jewish tradition and was to be done with a partner. We simply paired up with whoever was near. Those who were without partners raised their hands and found each other. Timothy taught the song and the steps to the dance, a couple demonstrated, we practiced singing, and then we began. Some moved hesitantly, at first losing the rhythm or getting the directions confused; others danced easily and with grace. Many sang, and a few danced silently. Even those simply watching participated in their own unique ways. Everyone was welcome, beginners were encouraged, and as the dance repeated over and over and over, all became more adept and at ease. As I flowed with the rhythm, and with the words "peace to everyone" on my lips and ringing in my ears, I became comfortable enough to look around. Everywhere I looked were people turning and swaying and singing and humming, all with peace on their minds and in their hearts. I felt exhilarated and part of something much larger than myself.

We continued throughout the evening with dances from a Native American tradition, the Sufi tradition, the Christian tradition, and a dance in celebration of the earth. All the dances were done in a circle, some with partners, some without. All the dances were repeated over and over and over again. I danced with women and men I had never met before, people of all ages and abilities. I sang some of the songs, listened to others, and alternately stumbled and flowed. The evening ended with a prayer of gratitude and an invitation to come back the following week and to bring our friends. I went out into the cold and moonlit night, still feeling the dances in my heart.

As I drove home slowly and quietly, I remembered a book I had read some years earlier, a book on Asian women's theology, titled *Struggle to Be the Sun Again,* by Chung Hyun Kyung. In this book, the author introduces the

Korean word *han*. "*Han* is the most prevalent feeling among Korean people who have been violated through their history by surrounding powerful countries."[12] The feeling of *han* can overwhelm and defeat a people, because it arises out of unresolved anger and resentment about years of oppression. But Korean women have brought their survival wisdom to bear on *han* and have found ways to untangle the webs of resentment. "In Korean tradition the untanglement of *han* is named *han-pu-ri*."[13]

Chung Hyun Kyung goes on to explain that there are two strands to *han-pu-ri*. One is the militant strand, which is expressed in organized political movements. The other strand is gentle *han-pu-ri*, which is expressed in ritual, dance, and song.[14] The two ways of *han-pu-ri* support and reinforce each other. Both ease the pain of injustice suffered and lead to new vision and new action in a hurtful and hurting world.

Han-pu-ri had been only a concept until the night I first danced the dances of universal peace. Now *han-pu-ri* was an experience, an experience of untangling resentment, an experience of hope, and an experience of renewal and community. However we pray, whether through work and service to others and all creation, through organizing action for justice and equality, or through dance and song, we are not praying alone. Let us celebrate all these ways to pray with body and soul.

ACTIVITIES FOR REFLECTION AND DISCUSSION

1. Become aware of and pay attention to the agitation around you and within you. Simply notice, without judgment, what is going on. Look for as wide a variety of experiences of agitation as possible. As you become more accustomed to recognizing agitation, begin to bring a contemplative quality into the situation. You might practice the breath prayer described in chapter 1 for a few moments. You might draw on the wisdom of Psalm 46:10, and repeat to yourself slowly "Be still, and know that I am God." Do not use these prayers to escape the agitation, but call on your relationship with God to bring focus and intention into your actions and to transform the situation.

2. Make a list of all the ways you could be compassionate toward yourself. Then make a list of all the ways you serve others or could serve others. Spend time with both lists and make some choices that will bring your life into balance. Pay attention to your tendency to go out of balance either toward yourself or toward service to others. Share your insights and decisions with your study group. As the group hears of others' areas of service, see if all are willing to support the service with prayers. As members share actions they will take out of compassion for themselves, see if these actions too can be supported by the prayers of others.

3. Remember a time when you acted for justice. What motivated your actions? How did you feel? What were the consequences of your actions? Remember all the complexities of the situation, the pressures, the fears, the insecurities. As you look back on the situation, is there anything you would do differently? Share your active prayers for justice with others in your group. Then ask yourself and each other if there is somewhere in your life right now that is calling you to act prayerfully for justice.

4. We often think we need to go to the country or the mountains or the beach to walk on the earth. Remember that when you walk on cement or asphalt or bricks you are still walking on the earth. Practice walking with the awareness that you are walking on the body of God. Explore ways of walking lightly, reverently, attending to each step. Imagine that each time your foot touches the ground you are deepening your relationship with God.

8

~~~

PRAYING TOGETHER
AS THE BODY OF CHRIST

Hearing the church called "the body of Christ" was very confusing to me as a child. My literal mind saw the body of Jesus feeding crowds of people, playing with children, riding a donkey, eating meals, being hung on a cross. How could the First Congregational Church of Palo Alto, California, be the body of Christ? Maybe the minister was the body of Christ. He was human. He had a body. But he was my friend's dad, someone who came to our house for dinner, and my parents called him by his first name. So his being the body of Christ did not make sense either.

This confusion did not get in the way of my enjoying going to church and being part of church. I loved the variety of people, the hymns and the prayers, the Bible stories and the projects. As I grew older, I assisted in teaching Sunday school for six-year-olds and became active in the youth group. I went to camp, participated in service projects, and learned what it meant to be a Christian. I began to understand that by calling the church "the body of Christ" we were saying that the church and all its members are the physical manifestation of the spirit of Christ. I was excited to be part of the body of Christ.

In my early twenties I was no longer excited. I felt that the church was not living up to its name. I was disillusioned by the denominational arguments and the hierarchy of church organization. I felt that the answers the church was providing were not aimed at the questions I was asking. I discovered that the images of God, Christ, heaven, kingdom, and salvation were so transcendent they had nothing to do with my daily life. I was taught in a college class that the Bible was not the word of God but a series of books authored by men, filled with history and stories and contradictions. And, most important, I came to believe that the church would not encourage me to become an individual—separate from my family, discover my own truths, find my own voice, and become my own person. I believed that the church wanted to keep me confined, while psychology and philosophy were urging me to grow. I did not believe I could become an individual and remain a Christian. So I left the church in favor of my individual journey.

For the next 20 years I wandered and explored. I found joy in my body through dancing, hiking, and body work. I found a deep connection to nature. I found peace in the practice of meditation. I found affirmation in the writings of women. I found hope in the study of transpersonal psychologies. I found community among like-minded seekers. I discovered I was a spiritual person. I discovered my soul. And I began to wonder about my Christian roots. Could my discoveries of these years be welcomed in the church? Were the teachings of Jesus so different from what I had come to believe about myself, about life, about others, about God? Because I was so afraid of joining a church that might force me to conform, I decided to continue my spiritual explorations at seminary.

During my years of study, I found that the true church did not demand obedience and conformity. I learned that Jesus encouraged us to move beyond the cultural norms and to question the accepted practices of a people. I learned that being a Christian meant discovering for myself my relationship with God and the risen Christ. And I learned that one cannot be a Christian alone.

As I recognized the truth of that last teaching, I resisted it, because I was still afraid that a local church would not be as inclusive as the image of church I had discovered in seminary. So I went looking for a congregation slowly and very carefully. I found a small church I liked, copastored by a husband and wife, and I began attending worship. I was careful not to become too involved. I shared little of myself. I was welcomed but not pursued. For two years I skulked around the edges of the congregation, slowly discovering not only that I could not be a Christian alone, I did not *want* to be a Christian alone. I was being called into community. When I was finally able to answer that call, I reaffirmed my Christian baptism and joined that local congregation on a beautiful Palm Sunday. I knew I had entered a new phase of my journey.

Becoming the Body of Christ

William Shannon, a Catholic priest, names what I was escaping in my twenties "collectivity." He calls what I was joining in my forties "community."[1] Although both of these groups may look similar to the outer observer, the experience of members of either group is vastly different. The member of a collectivity is expected to uphold the belief system of the group at whatever cost to individual questions, concerns, or doubts. At times, this expectation can provide safety and reassurance to the individual. Answers are provided for questions, membership is affirmed, and harmony exists among people who all think and believe alike. At other times, the expectation of the collectivity feels stifling and confining, with no space to breathe, move, explore, or experience. A conflict emerges between staying/fitting in and escaping/being alone.

True community offers another alternative to its members, the possibility of "belonging to" rather than "fitting in." Community welcomes the seeker and is open to individual differences. Community asks its members to bring their own unique gifts for the good of the community and provides a freedom for individual expression. Community expects personal responsibility, creativity, and accountability from its members, which can lead to disagreement and dissension. Belonging to a community can be difficult as well as rewarding.

When we are young, the experience of collectivity can be nourishing because it provides safety and affirmation that we are not alone. We fit in; we know what is expected; we do not need to concern ourselves with personal beliefs and responsibilities. As we mature we may long for more than safety and fitting in. We may desire new connections and seek out different opportunities and possibilities. Often we thrive on new and exciting experiences, but as we pursue our own way in the world, we realize that we are not meant to be alone. We recognize our need to belong, and we search for true community.

I recently read a poem written by Symeon the New Theologian in the eleventh century. His writing adds a different dimension to the meaning of true community and to becoming and being the body of Christ.

> We awaken in Christ's body
> as Christ awakens our bodies,
> and my poor hand is Christ, He enters
> my foot, and is infinitely me.
>
> I move my hand, and wonderfully
> my hand becomes Christ, becomes all of Him
> (for God is indivisibly
> whole, seamless in His Godhood).
>
> I move my foot, and at once
> He appears like a flash of lightning.
> Do my words seem blasphemous? — Then
> open your heart to Him
>
> and let yourself receive the one
> who is opening to you so deeply.
> For if we genuinely love Him,
> we wake up inside Christ's body

> where all our body, all over,
> every most hidden part of it,
> is realized in joy as Him,
> and He makes us, utterly, real,
>
> and everything that is hurt, everything
> that seemed to us dark, harsh, shameful,
> maimed, ugly, irreparably
> damaged, is in Him transformed
>
> and recognized as whole, as lovely,
> and radiant in His light
> we awaken as the beloved
> in every last part of our body.[2]

In this imagery, *I* am the body of Christ; *you* are the body of Christ; each person is the body of Christ as well as all being members of the body of Christ. This imagery affirms for us the sacred nature of the individual as well as the sacred nature of the community. This imagery helps us see the difference in Christian terms between a collectivity and a community. A collectivity might proclaim: "We are the body of Christ!" but not encourage the awakening of the individual into Christ's body, nor welcome the person who comes already clothed in the body of Christ. A community, on the other hand, understands its important role to be a midwife for the birthing of the person who can individually take on the body of Christ. This person then freely joins with others to be the body of Christ, which is called to manifest physically the spirit of Christ in the world today.

The Imperfect Body of Christ

During seminary, when I overcame my resistance to organized Christianity and joined my local congregation, I went "in care" with the United Church of Christ. This action said to the church that I was considering the possibility of ordination and that I was grounded in a faith community as well as pursuing my studies. In turn, by being taken in care, the wider church said to me that they would support and nurture me as I discerned my call to the ordained ministry. As I became more sure of my Christian faith, as I became comfortable calling myself a Christian, as I became more active in my local church, I realized that I was not called to parish ministry, but to a special ministry of teaching and spiritual direction. As I wrote papers, took examinations, participated in discussion, and prayed, the In Care Committee affirmed my call. All seemed to be in place, but something stood in my way.

I finally recognized that the resistance I had to being ordained was that I was not in full harmony with the body of Christ. I had many quarrels with the Christian Church. I was appalled by the violence of the Crusades and the Inquisition. I was disgusted by the politics and infighting and jockeying for power that were so rampant in various periods of our history. I was saddened by the opulence and wealth of the church in times when so many were and are in need of the basics for survival. I was deeply hurt by the ways the church had degraded and excluded women. I was amazed at the vicious way some members of the body of Christ were treating other members of the body of Christ. How could I become not only a member but a spokesperson, a representative, an official leader of this deeply flawed institution?

Over time and with the help of classmates and professors, I realized I was longing for a "perfect" church. I was amazed at myself, and a little embarrassed, because I had known for a long time that people were not called to perfection but to wholeness. How could I have overlooked the fact that the church also was not called to perfection but to wholeness? For the church, as well as for people, perfection was not the issue. When I saw the church in process of becoming, I was willing to join the process and contribute what gifts I had to making the church more able to reflect a just and loving image of God. I also knew that if I were to continue my process of becoming I needed to belong to this lively, arguing, imperfect community. So I accepted my call and I was ordained to the Christian ministry of the United Church of Christ in 1987 in my local congregation, surrounded by family and friends.

Just as our imperfect bodies need our prayers, not to become perfect but to become whole in the midst of imperfection, so the church, the body of Christ, needs our prayers. The church needs prayers for its healing and its transformation and the church also needs pray-ers in the midst of its struggle to be a spiritual community. The following story demonstrates how wounds in the body of Christ can be healed through prayer.

A local congregation was in turmoil over the selection of their new pastor. A search committee had been selected to represent the many groups within the congregation. They had been approved by the congregation and empowered by the polity of the church. But there were members of the church council who did not want the committee to function independently, so they began to manipulate the search process. The young associate pastor was caught in the middle.

This woman had become the associate before the previous senior pastor had resigned. When he left, she had applied to become the interim pastor for the congregation. She was told that because many in her congregation hoped she would become their new pastor, her application for interim was denied.

According to church policy, interim pastors are not allowed to apply for the permanent position. So she retained the position of associate during the tenure of the interim minister and tried to discern whether she felt a call to put her name in for the senior position.

During this time she became aware that some of the council members did not want her to be senior pastor. They did not want her to apply, because the final selection would be out of their control. Many members of the congregation became aware of the manipulation, and the church divided against itself.

"If I apply for the position and receive it," she mused to her prayer group, "I'll become the pastor of many who do not want me there, and the division will continue. If I do not apply, even though I feel called, I will be compromising my integrity. But by not applying, the church congregation might end its division and come back together." The group joined with her in silent prayer about her dilemma. In the discussion that followed the time of prayer, someone said: "If you do not apply, your congregation might reconcile, but the body of Christ will not be healed. The struggle for power, the deceit, and the manipulation will remain." The woman thanked the group for their prayers and their listening hearts. She said she would continue praying until a decision was reached.

A month later, she reported to her prayer group what had happened. Through prayer, she had discerned that she was called to apply to be senior pastor to that congregation. When she put her name forward, the council members who did not want her began to manipulate the selection process. Their disregard for established procedure became apparent. They were lovingly and firmly informed that their behavior would not be tolerated. The search committee placed her name with the name of other candidates and then spent many days in discussion and hours in prayer about who would be the best person to lead the congregation. Their discernment led them to select one of the other applicants.

"How do you feel about that?" one of her concerned prayer partners asked. "Well," she replied with a slow smile, "my ego has a mosquito bite on it, but other than that, I am truly fine with the decision, because I know it came from prayer. The search committee reached consensus and were in full agreement about one of the other candidates. I trust their individual and group process. I believe that through prayer and discernment the final decision was God's. I will stay on for a while as associate pastor, and then, who knows. But for now, the congregation has begun to heal, and for that I am grateful. I know some of my supporters will be disappointed, but because I am comfortable with the outcome, I can guide them to acceptance."

The body of Christ is healed by prayers and pray-ers. And yet this healing is not always obvious to those outside the church, who often see the church as riddled with conflict and power struggles. As we heal ourselves we can become visible pray-ers beyond our local congregations. People of the world need to experience Christians who pray with body and soul in public, making our faith, hope, and compassion more visible in a broken world.

The Labyrinth and the Church

The labyrinth is an ancient spiritual tool that can guide us in our prayer and also help us form images of the church as a true spiritual community. The diagram below is a representation of the labyrinth found in the nave of Chartres Cathedral in France. This labyrinth is forty-one feet wide and dates from 1220. The Reverend Dr. Lauren Artress, canon for special ministries at Grace Cathedral in San Francisco, California, started the Labyrinth Project in 1991, after visiting Chartres and walking the labyrinth. Her own profound experience of the holy led her to discover a way to make the labyrinth available to many people. Dr. Artress produced a canvas labyrinth to be used in Grace Cathedral, and then designed a "seed kit," which gives instructions for others to make their own labyrinths. The labyrinth, and the practice of walking it is becoming available in more and more places in this country.[3]

Walking the labyrinth is a prayer form symbolizing our walk with God and our walk toward God. Some people walk with a verbal prayer on their lips or in their hearts. Others hold a question or a petition and open themselves to hearing an answer or receiving an insight. Others walk simply for fun and relaxation, and still others walk to be energized. The experience of walking the labyrinth is different for everyone, and often very different for the same person every time it is walked.

I walked the labyrinth for the first time at Grace Cathedral during a Lenten retreat. I was nervous about the experience, not knowing what to expect. I had been assured that I could not get lost because the labyrinth is made up of a single winding path which leads you to the center and then leads you back out again. The labyrinth is not a maze, which is designed to trick you by sending you on detours and trapping you in dead ends.[4] I

was still apprehensive, wondering what would occur on this sacred path.

"Whatever occurs on the Labyrinth is a metaphor," Dr. Artress told us before we began. "If you get annoyed at others on the path, treat that awareness as a metaphor for your life. If you resist traveling toward the center or resist returning, understand that awareness as a metaphor."

I decided to walk the labyrinth simply for the experience and to be attentive to whatever happened in the process. My nervousness turned to anticipation as I stepped onto the canvas and began my journey. The first thing I noticed was that I was very quickly close to the center although I knew I still had a long way to go before I arrived. I then became aware that I could not tell exactly where I was in relation to the beginning or the end, and there was no way for me to look forward and plan my route. Because I tend to anticipate the future in many areas of my life, I found this inability to plan ahead disconcerting. But I also recognized the freedom of simply attending to the moment—my steps, the patterns on the floor, the movements of others, and my body in motion.

I began to relax and appreciate everyone's intention and the stillness in the midst of movement. I began to look at the people I passed who were going at a slower pace, and those who I met who were on their return journey. Occasionally I would step off the path at a resting spot and simply watch the beauty of the process.

I lost track of time. I had no idea how long I had been walking. I began to think that I should reach the center soon, but I didn't reach it. I just kept walking, following the path before me. I began to get disoriented with all the twists and turns. I felt anxious, but reminded myself that I just needed to keep walking. So, I breathed deeply a couple of times, continued moving, and arrived at the entrance!

The entrance! What a surprise! What a disappointment! I had finished my journey without ever reaching the center! What had happened? What had I done wrong? How had I gotten lost on a single path? And then I began to laugh. If whatever happened on the labyrinth was a metaphor for life, I had just been given a glorious insight. How often I wish for an "arrival" in the spiritual life. How often I forsake the journey for the destination. How often I assume I have done something wrong if I do not meet my expectations. How often I get lost even when I believe I have one true path in my mind and heart.

I sat down to reflect on all that had happened, and when I felt clearer, I started walking the labyrinth once again. This time I felt like I was floating, freed of worry and anticipation. I was simply walking, moving, opening all my senses to the full experience. This time I did reach the center, but the "arrival" felt more like a stop along the way rather than an end point or a goal attained. Arriving was simply part of the process of walking with and toward God, part of my journey of body and soul.

I realized that my own practice of prayer was enhanced because of the insights I received by walking the sacred path, but I did not realize the labyrinth's rich potential for community until I introduced it to my prayer class. A local group had made a portable labyrinth, which they were willing to loan to interested groups. They brought it to the seminary where I teach, and one of their leaders presented the historical and theological background of the labyrinth to my prayer class. She also explained the Christian and pre-Christian symbolism contained in the labyrinth.[5] She then invited the students onto the path to experience it for themselves.

To support the process, I went to the edge of the labyrinth and prayerfully watched as student after student began walking. The students walked at very different speeds. Some had their hands folded over their hearts, others walked with hands behind their backs. One woman moved her arms as if she were flying. A student invited a young child to accompany her, another spent some time walking backward. As all these diverse students walked in their own unique ways, the labyrinth began to fill. I was astounded to realize that I had no way of knowing who was coming and who was going, who had arrived and who had just begun. I watched as students seemed to walk for a moment in step with one another, and then one would turn back and the other would continue on. Sometimes it appeared that students were moving against each other, going in opposite directions, and then as they were about to collide, one would step aside and the other would glide by.

I sat in awe of the beautiful, flowing, vibrant image of the body of Christ that was before me. I was witnessing a community in prayer and action. Everyone was walking the same path, but traveling with the freedom to walk as they wished. No one was above or below, ahead or behind. Everyone was simply moving with and toward God, and with each other. "An image of the church," I breathed. "A healed and whole and holy church."

The Soul of the Church

Prayer awakens the soul of the body of Christ. Without prayer, a congregation is only a building, an organization, or an institution that may function well, do good works, care for its people. But without prayer, a church has no vibrancy, no imagination, no vision—no soul. The church without soul is like the observatory without its telescope.

As we long to bring all of ourselves, body and soul, to God, we long to bring all of who we are to a soulful community. Our souls yearn for communion with other souls in a society we often experience as soulless. As we learn to pray with body and soul and bring our prayers together in the church, the church will begin to experience its own soul.

An urban church in Denver, Colorado, decided one Lenten season to cancel all their church meetings. In place of the meetings, prayer and study groups were scheduled to which all members of the congregation were invited. The groups were held six times during each week to accommodate everyone's schedule. There were three early morning groups, one noon group, and two evening groups. Each group met five times between Ash Wednesday and Palm Sunday.

The church leadership chose *Prayer: Beginning Conversations with God* for all the groups to study.[6] They believed that if everyone read and studied and prayed with the same material, a connection would build not only within each group but among the groups. And that's what happened! As the congregation read and studied and prayed together and alone, people experienced prayer at the center of their individual lives. They experienced prayer at the center of their communal lives. By organizing themselves around prayer rather than business, this congregation created a soulful community.

Another Denver congregation, this one in the suburbs, responded to the longings for prayer in their congregation by holding a "prayer sampler." The church leadership knew that their members were eager to pray and were asking for information and guidelines to help them. To accommodate the diversity of needs and interests, the sampler was designed to introduce participants to twelve different aspects of prayer. Leaders from their own congregation planned half-hour presentations on a variety of topics, such as "Prayer and Movement," "Centering Prayer," "Praying with Children," "Praying Aloud," and "Praying the Psalms." Four sessions were held simultaneously so people had a choice among the offerings.

The congregation gathered after worship for a potluck lunch and fellowship. Then with great excitement they began their exploration of prayer. Choices were difficult to make because so much was being offered. Families split up so they could taste and sample a wider variety of prayer and share at home what they had learned. The short presentation time kept people's interest, and the grouping and regrouping built prayerful connections among the church members. Many people said that the prayer sampler gave them new ideas that deepened their relationship to God. Others experienced the festival as a turning point for their congregation because of the many people who were able to come together to learn to pray.

Just as these churches created ways to involve their members in prayer, all congregations can find ways to become more soulful. I believe the body of Christ needs more creativity, more prayer, more dancing, more story-

telling, more laughter. The church needs more diverse relationships with all
peoples and all of creation. To awaken its soul, the church needs more experience of the sacred in daily living. As we pray together with body and soul,
the whole church can become more open to the presence of the living God
among us. The church needs us, body and soul, so we can grow together in
wholeness. Together, in partnership with the God in whom we live and move
and have our being, we can bring alive the soul in the body of Christ.

ACTIVITIES FOR REFLECTION AND DISCUSSION

1. What is your "church story"? Did you grow up in the church in which
you are still a member? Did you leave for a while and return? Did you ever
go "church shopping"? Are you avoiding church involvement? Are you
searching for the perfect church? Does an understanding of the difference
between a collectivity and a community help you understand any movement
you have had away from the church or toward the church? If you are in a
discussion group, share your church stories with one another.

2. Write a prayer for the healing of the church. You might begin with
something like this:

> Gracious and loving God, in whom all things are possible—We know that
> the body of Christ is not all it can be. We know that it is broken and
> wounded in many ways. We know that the brokenness comes from our
> own brokenness. Heal us, love us, empower us to transform your church
> so that it becomes a reflection of your love for all the world.
>
> In the name of the one who gave His life that we might become the
> body of Christ, Amen.

Add your own petitions for the healing of your own local church, being specific about the wounds with which it struggles, such as division, apathy, confusion, emptiness, lack of mission. Pray for courage and strength to become
a member who can help to heal the body of Christ.

3. Is your church a community of pray-ers? How do members pray individually and together? Is there some way that your church could become
more intentional in its prayer life, such as beginning a prayer chain or gathering in prayer groups, holding a workshop on prayer or sponsoring a day of
prayer? Are you willing to guide others toward awakening the soul of your
church? Discuss the many ways your church could become more soulful.

GROUP STUDY GUIDE

Praying with Body and Soul can be read and explored as a group in ten sessions. These sessions may be weekly or monthly, depending on the structure and the tradition of the study group.

Each session is designed with an opening activity to gather people around an experience of prayer. Following the initial sharing are questions to help group members integrate the material of the book into their own prayer lives. One or two activities are then suggested for the group to do together. Each session ends with both an invitation to engage in prayer between meetings and a reading assignment with a suggested activity to prepare the group for the following session.

Some groups may wish to begin and end with prayer. Some groups will spend a whole session on one question or one activity, and others will touch lightly on many. Some groups enjoy sharing in pairs or triads, while others prefer all sharing to be with the total group. Hold the session outlines lightly and follow the lead of the group and the movement of the Spirit. There is nowhere to go and nothing to be accomplished besides coming together to be with each other and with God.

Session One

Opening: Share your names and what draws you to the study of prayer. Discuss the structure of the group and decide on meeting times and places.

Questions: How were you taught to pray? Who taught you? Do you remember early childhood prayers? What did you learn about the nature of prayer? Who was the God to whom you were praying?

Activity: Pass out the books and read the Introduction aloud together. Invite participants to reflect on what has guided them beyond their early understanding of prayer, whether they have ever experienced the "wooing" of God, and how their prayer might change if they brought all of themselves to God.

Homework: Attend to the ways God calls you into prayer, the ways of God's "wooing." Read chapter 1. Practice the breath prayer on pages 12–13 and move one of the biblical passages described in the text or listed in activity #3, chapter 1.

Session Two

Opening: Share what your bodies taught you about prayer through the different prayer positions, the breath prayer, or moving a biblical passage.

Questions: What body movement helps you pray? What prayer phrase would be your own personal prayer of the heart? Have you ever treated your body as an enemy? What one thing could you do to befriend your body? Give examples. What happens to your body when you watch liturgical dance?

Activity: #3 or #4, chapter 1.

Homework: Pay attention to your bodies as teachers of prayer. Read chapter 2. Do the "Knowing God" activity on page 27.

Session Three

Opening: Share the many ways you know God through your senses.

Questions: How could opening your senses expand your prayer life? When and how has God grabbed your attention? Do you remember an early sensual prayer? How is music a prayer for you? What in your life is praying by hand?

Activity: #3, chapter 2.

Homework: Practice "this too speaks of God," as described on page 30. Read chapter 3. Reflect on times in your own life when your body betrayed you. How did you pray?

Session Four

Opening: Share your responses to the five stories of body betrayal and prayer.

Questions: Do you remember ways your body betrayed you as a child? As a teenager? How does your body betray you as you are aging? What prayers have helped you through times of betrayal by the body? How might you pray for and with your body to help it become your friend? Can you imagine treating death as a friend?

Activity: #3, chapter 3.

Homework: Watch for images of wholeness in your daily lives. Read chapter 4. Do activity #1.

Session Five

Opening: Share the humorous aspects of creation you have discovered and any prayers you have fashioned.

Questions: When has laughter and play brought you closer to God? What is your image of God laughing? Have you ever been hurt by laughter? How might you take your hurt into prayer? How and when are you a clown? How might you be a fool for God?

Activity: #2, chapter 4.

Homework: Watch for and create opportunities to laugh and play with God. Read chapter 5. Do activity #1.

Session Six

Opening: Share your images and speak about how these images guide you in prayer.

Questions: Was your imagination affirmed and encouraged as a child? How do you exercise your imagination? What is your image of the soul? What vivid dream images do you remember? How might they guide you in prayer?

Activity: #2, #3, or #5, chapter 5.

Homework: Create one or more prayer drawings or sculptures. Read chapter 6. Do activity #1.

Session Seven

Opening: Share your prayer drawings. Share the many ways you name yourself.

Questions: How does it feel to think of yourself as rich and complex and multifaceted? Can you identify how some of your many parts like to pray? What are some of your blocks to prayer? What do you need to include in your prayer life to experience a rich and pregnant holiness? What person in a Bible story do you identify with? How can that person's story guide you in prayer?

Activity: #3, chapter 6.

Homework: Practice including your interruptions in your prayer. Read chapter 7. Do activity #2.

Session Eight

Opening: Share your reflections on compassion and service.

Questions: When have you experienced prayerful action? When have you been an active contemplative? How is your work a prayer? How have you prayed for peace? When have you acted for justice? How do you belong to the earth?

Activity: #3, chapter 7.

Homework: Practice walking lightly, reverently on the earth. Read chapter 8. Do activity #1.

Session Nine

Opening: Share your church stories.

Questions: When have you tried to "fit in"? What did it do to your soul? When have you had the experience of belonging? What does it feel like to imagine that *you* are the body of Christ? How does that feeling guide your prayer? Where do you experience wounds in your church? How might you help to heal these wounds? What would it mean to you personally if the soul of the body of Christ were awakened?

Activity: #2, chapter 8.

Homework: Continue to pray for the church and your own congregation. Reflect on activity #3, chapter 8.

Session Ten

Opening: How is your church a community of pray-ers?

Questions: What one idea, or experience, or activity has expanded your practice of prayer? How have the sharings of others in the group influenced your understanding of prayer? How will you continue your practice of prayer? Are you willing to talk to others about your prayer life? What ideas do you have about bringing prayer more intentionally into your congregation?

Activity: Have a closing celebration. Share a meal. Play a game. Do a guided meditation. Have a prayer service. Serve communion.

Homework: Remember that faithfulness in prayer is the willingness to always start over!

NOTES

Introduction

1. Mitchell, Stephen, A *Book of Psalms: Selected and Adapted from the Hebrew* (New York: HarperCollins, 1993) p. 71.

2. "The Heidelberg Catechism," *The Book of Confessions* (New York: PCUSA Office of the General Assembly, 1983) section 4.001.

Chapter 1: Our Bodies Teach Us to Pray

1. Bacovcin, Helen, *The Way of a Pilgrim and The Pilgrim Continues His Way* (New York: Doubleday, 1992).

2. May, Gerald G., M.D., *Addiction and Grace* (San Francisco, Harper & Row, 1988).

3. Heuer, Holly, "The Bell Tower," Nederland Community Presbyterian Church, Vol. 13, No. 10, October 1, 1996.

4. DeSola, Carla, "Center for Women and Religion Membership Newsletter," Graduate Theological Union, Berkeley, Calif., Nov./Dec., 1996, p. 5.

Chapter 2: Our Sexuality and Sensuality Help Us Know God

1. Moltman, Jürgen, *The Spirit of Life: A Universal Affirmation,* Translated by Margaret Kohl from the German (Minneapolis: Fortress Press, 1985) p. 331.

2. Thich Nhat Hanh, *A Guide to Walking Meditation,* Translated by Jenny Hoang and Anh Huong (New Haven: Eastern Press, 1985).

3. Hildegard of Bingen, cited in *The Quotable Woman,* ed. Elaine Partnow (New York, Bicester: Facts On File Publications, 1985) Section 163:12, p. 48.

4. Ann Stoenner, personal correspondence, September 1997.

5. Pennington, M. Basil, *Praying by Hand* (San Francisco: HarperCollins, 1991) p. 4.

6. Weber, Christine, "Fashioning a New Setting for an Ancient Treasure," *National Catholic Reporter*, December 13, 1996, p. 16.

7. Whitehead, Evelyn Eaton and James D., *A Sense of Sexuality: Christian Love and Intimacy* (New York: Doubleday, 1989) pp. 40–41.

8. Nelson, James B., *Humanly Speaking: A Foundation Paper on Human Identity, Relationship and Sexuality* (Cleveland: United Church Board for Homeland Ministries, 1995) p. 15.

9. Whitehead, p. 24.

10. Ibid.

11. Bonhoeffer, Dietrich, *Letters and Papers from Prison*, enlarged edition, edited by Eberhard Bethge (New York: MacMillan Co., 1953, 1971) p. 303.

12. Bancroft, Alan, *St. Therese of Lisieux* (London: Harper Collins, 1996) p. xiii.

13. Ibid., p. 110.

14. Kavanaugh, Kieran, O.C.D. and Otilo Rodriquez, editors, *The Collected Works of St. John of the Cross* (Washington, D.C.: ICS Publications, 1973) p. 413.

15. Ibid., p. 296.

16. Robinson, Constance, *Passion and Marriage* (London: SPCK., 1965) p. 75.

Chapter 3: Praying When Our Bodies Betray Us

1. Conroy, Frank, *Body and Soul* (Boston: Houghton Mifflin, 1993) p. 33.

2. Bernardin, Joseph Cardinal, *Gift of Peace* (Chicago: Loyola Press, 1997) p. 68.

3. Ibid., pp. 67–68.

4. Ibid., p. 126.

5. Ibid., p. 126.

6. Nouwen, Henry J.M., *Inner Voice of Love: A Journey through Anguish to Freedom* (New York: Doubleday, 1996) p. 19.

7. Eiesland, Nancy L., *The Disabled God: Toward a Liberating Theology of Disability* (Nashville: Abingdon Press, 1994) p. 100.

8. Remen, Rachel Naomi, cited in *Life Prayers From Around the World*, ed. Elizabeth Roberts and Elias Amidon (San Francisco: HarperCollins, 1996) p. 270.

Chapter 4: Humor, Laughter, and Playful Prayer

1. Hyers, Conrad, *The Comic Vision and the Christian Faith: A Celebration of Life and Laughter* (New York: Pilgrim Press, 1981) p. 15.

2. Liebenow, Mark, *Is There Fun After Paul?: A Theology of Clowning* (San Jose: Resource Publications) p. 43.

3. Ibid., pp. 1–2.

4. Bernardo, Rick. "A Serious Meditation on Laughter," *Evangelion*, Pacific School of Religion, Fall 1981, p. 15.

5. Mullen, Tom, *Laughing Out Loud and Other Religious Experiences* (Waco: Word Book Publishers, 1983) p. 43.

6. Willimon, William H., *And the Laugh Shall Be First* (Nashville: Abingdon Press, 1986) p. 10.

7. Forster, E.M., *A Passage to India* (San Diego: Harcourt Brace and Company, 1924) p. 324.

8. Cox, Harvey, *The Feast of Fools: A Theological Essay in Festivity and Fantasy* (Cambridge, Mass.: Harvard University Press, 1969) p. 3.

9. Ibid., pp. 3–4.

10. Liebenow, p. 7.

11. Ibid., p. 7.

12. Ibid., p. 4.

13. Willimon, p. 9.

Chapter 5: Praying with Our Imaginations

1. *Webster's New Collegiate Dictionary* (Springfield, Mass.: G. and C. Merriam, 1953) p. 414.

2. Moore, Alvin, Jr., "The Noble Traveler," *Parabola: Myth, Tradition, and the Search for Meaning,* Summer 1996, p. 6.

3. Roethke, Theodore, "The Restored," *The Collected Poems of Theodore Roethke* (Garden City, N.Y.: Anchor Press/Doubleday, 1975) p. 241.

4. Moore, p. 7.

5. Wright, Wendy M., "Living Into the Image: Thoughts on Religious Imagination and the Images of Tradition," *Weavings,* Jan./Feb., 1997, Vol. 12, No. 1, p. 9.

6. Ibid., p. 9.

7. Sanford, John A., *Dreams and Healing: A Succinct and Lively Interpretation of Dreams* (New York: Paulist Press, 1978) p. 7.

8. Vennard, Jane E., "Guided by Dreams," *Journal of Women and Religion* (Berkeley: Center for Women and Religion, 1988) pp. 52–60.

9. Bondi, Roberta C., *In Ordinary Time: Healing the Wounds of the Heart* (Nashville: Abingdon Press, 1996) p. 22.

10. Ibid.

Chapter 6: Our Many Selves Guide Us in Prayer

1. Nouwen, Henri J. M., *The Inner Voice of Love: A Journey Through Anguish to Freedom* (New York: Doubleday, 1996) p. 78.

2. Ibid., pp. 78–79.

3. Sanford, John A., *The Kingdom Within: The Inner Meaning of Jesus' Sayings* (San Francisco: Harper and Row, Publishers, 1987) p. 136.

Chapter 7: Action Prayers: Work, Service, Justice, and Care of the Earth

1. Chittester, Joan, O.S.B., *Wisdom Distilled From the Daily: Living the Rule of St. Benedict Today* (New York: HarperCollins, 1990) p. 84.

2. Ibid., p. 85.

3. Ibid.

4. Ibid., p. 86.

5. Palmer, Parker J., *The Active Life* (New York: Harper Collins, 1991) p. 122.

6. Kornfield, Jack, *A Path With Heart: A Guide through the Perils and Promises of Spiritual Life* (New York: Bantam Books, 1993) p. 225.

7. Borg, Marcus J., *The God We Never Know: Beyond Dogmatic Religion to a More Authentic Contemporary Faith* (New York: HarperCollins, 1997) p. 32.

8. Appletree Press, editor, *A Little Book of Irish Verse* (Belfast: The Appletree Press, 1991) p. 7.

9. McFague, Sallie, *The Body of God: an Ecological Theology* (Minneapolis: Fortress Press, 1993) p. viii.

10. Ibid., p. xi.

11. For information about the Dances for Universal Peace and to find one near you, contact:

> Peace Works
> International Center for The Dances of Universal Peace
> 444 E. Ravenna Blvd., Ste. 306
> Seattle, WA 98115-5487
> (206) 522-4353

12. Kyung, Chung Hyun, *Struggle to Be the Sun Again* (Maryknoll, N.Y.: Orbis Books, 1990) p. 42.

13. Ibid., p. 43.

14. Ibid., p. 43.

Chapter 8: Praying Together as the Body of Christ

1. Shannon, William H., *Seeking the Face of God* (New York: Crossroad Publishing Company, 1988) pp. 139–41.

2. Mitchell, Stephen, editor, *The Enlightened Heart* (New York: Harper & Row, 1988) pp. 38–39.

3. Artress, Dr. Lauren, *Walking a Sacred Path: Rediscovering the Labyrinth as a Sacred Tool* (New York: Riverhead Books, 1995) pp. 180–83.

4. Aviva, Elyn, "The Amazing Labyrinth," *The World and I*, September 1997, p. 183.

5. For a full explanation of the symbols of the labyrinth, see Artress, chapter 8, pp. 45–46.

6. Beckman, Richard J., *Prayer: Beginning Conversations with God* (Minneapolis: Augsburg Books, 1995).

FOR FURTHER READING

Chapter 1: Our Bodies Teach Us to Pray

DeSola, Carla, *The Spirit Moves: A Handbook of Dance and Prayer* (Berkeley: Sharing Co., 1977, 1990)

May, Melanie A., *A Body Knows: A Theopoetics of Death and Resurrection* (New York: Continuum, 1995)

Porter, Phil with Winton-Henry, Cynthia, *Having It All: Body, Mind, Heart and Spirit: Together at Last* (Oakland: Wing It! Press, 1997)

Roth, Gabrielle, *Sweat Your Prayers: Movement as Spiritual Practice* (New York: Jeremy P. Tarcher/Putnam, 1997)

Wuellner, Flora Slosson, *Prayer and Our Bodies* (Nashville: The Upper Room, 1987)

Chapter 2: Our Sexuality and Sensuality Help Us Know God

Mollenkott, Virginia Ramey, *Sensuous Spirituality: Out from Fundamentalism* (New York: Crossroad, 1992)

Weber, Christin Lore, *Circle of Mysteries: The Women's Rosary Book,* (St. Paul: Yes International Publishers, 1995)

Chapter 3: Praying When Our Bodies Betray Us

Beckman, Richard J., *Praying for Wholeness and Healing* (Minneapolis: Augsburg Books, 1995)

Dossey, Larry, M.D., *Healing Words: The Power of Prayer and the Practice of Medicine* (San Francisco: HarperCollins, 1993)

Chapter 4: Humor, Laughter, and Playful Prayer

Hyers, Conrad, *And God Created Laughter: The Bible as Divine Comedy* (Atlanta: John Knox Press, 1987)

Shaffer, Floyd, *Clown Ministry Skits for All Seasons* (Loveland, Colo.: Group Books, 1990)

Chapter 5: Praying with Our Imaginations

Bergan, J. S., and Schwan, M., *Praying with Ignatius of Loyola* (Winona, Minn.: St. Mary's Press, 1997)

Coffey, Kathy, *Hidden Women of the Gospels* (New York: The Crossroad Publishing Company, 1996)

Linn, Dennis, Linn, Sheila Fabricant, and Linn, Matthew, *Good Goats: Healing Our Image of God* (Mahwah, New York: Paulist Press, 1994)

Sanford, John A., *Dreams: God's Forgotten Language* (New York: Crossroad, 1984)

Wink, Walter, *Transforming Bible Study: A Leader's Guide* (Nashville: Abingdon Press, 1989)

Chapter 6: Our Many Selves Guide Us in Prayer

Brown, Molly Young, *Growing Whole: Self-Realization on an Endangered Planet* (New York: HarperCollins, 1993)

Miller, William A., *Your Golden Shadow: Discovering and Fulfilling Your Undeveloped Self* (San Francisco: Harper & Row, 1989)

Chapter 7: Action Prayers: Work, Service, Justice, and Care of the Earth

Boyer, Ernest, Jr., *Finding God at Home: Family Life as Spiritual Discipline* (San Francisco: HarperCollins, 1984)

Gutierrez, Gustavo, *We Drink from Our Own Wells: The Spiritual Journey of a People* (Maryknoll, New York: Orbis Books, 1984)

Palmer, Parker J., *The Active Life: Wisdom for Work, Creativity and Caring* (San Francisco: HarperCollins, 1990)

Chapter 8: Praying Together as the Body of Christ

Mead, Loren B., *The Once and Future Church: Reinventing the Congregation for a New Mission Frontier* (Bethesda, Md.: The Alban Institute, 1991)